what is
goth
?

First published in 2004 by
Red Wheel/Weiser, LLC
York Beach, ME
With offices at:
368 Congress Street
Boston, MA 02210
www.redwheelweiser.com

LIBRARY OF CONGRESS CATALOGING-IN-PUBLICATION DATA
Voltaire.
  What is goth? / Voltaire.
     p. cm.
  ISBN 1-57863-322-2 (alk. paper)
  1. Goth culture (Subculture) I. Title.
  HQ796.V67 2004
  306'.1—dc22

                                        2004008833

Typeset in Adobe Garamond Semibold by Anne Carter

Printed in Canada
FR

11 10 09 08 07 06 05 04
  8 7 6 5 4 3 2 1

The paper used in this publication meets the minimum requirements of
the American National Standard for Information Sciences—Permanence
of Paper for Printed Library Materials Z39.48-1992 (R1997).

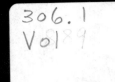

what is goth ?

voltaire

www.voltaire.net

table of contents

A Long-winded and self-aggrandizing introduction by the author

(Read this while I go pretend to kill myself.)

ONCE UPON A TIME, SOMEWHERE AROUND 1979, THE SUBGENRE OF PUNK MUSIC CALLED GOTHIC ROCK WAS BEING BORN IN LONDON. AT THAT TIME I WAS A CURIOUS, TWELVE-YEAR-OLD lad growing up in the purgatorial suburban sprawl of West Orange, New Jersey. Unlike most of my peers, I was drawn to the exotic and loathed the mundane existence that was (and presumably still is) life in an American suburb. I was also—like so many millions of other lads—somewhat disenfranchised and thus quickly developing a rather misanthropic outlook on life.

By the early '80s, Goth (along with its cousins, the New Wave, Industrial, and New Romantic scenes) had established itself suffi-ciently enough to start washing up on American shores. Back then I was something of an insomniac, preferring to sleep during daytime and spending many a night sneaking TV into the early-morning hours. Given these circumstances, it's no surprise that I was instant-ly enthralled when I turned on the TV at 4 AM one day and saw an Englishman (whose name I later learned was Adam Ant) prancing about in an elaborate eighteenth-century costume. It was a school night, and if the mere act of turning on the television wasn't taboo enough, there before me was a sight absolutely and completely alien to the world I knew. I was glued to the set with all of the mischie-vous glee of a Gothic monkey in a black leather banana factory.

The show I saw was *Night Flight*—a late-night, four-hour block of programming that included a feature-length horror film, animat-ed shorts, and music videos from England for songs that would never be played on mainstream American radio (at least not for another twenty years). Thus, I was introduced to the wide world of related musical genres: Goth, New Wave, Industrial, and such. That night, Siouxsie and the Banshees and the Cure crawled across my TV screen in their spooky-Kabuki makeup; Bauhaus followed, singing their trademark song—which has become the possibly indisputable anthem of the Goth scene—"Bela Lugosi's Dead." Then came the feature presentation, which was (surprise, surprise) *Dracula*, featuring you-know-who in the title role.

And then, of course, there was Adam Ant. I was then ignorant to the fact that he was on the New Romantic rather than the Gothic Rock end of the British musical spectrum; regardless, I was instantly hooked by his outlandish appearance and behavior. "Stand and deliver!" yelled the gaily clad, English dandy in his tricornered hat as he held up a stagecoach in a music video for a song of the same name. He oozed sexuality in a way I had never before seen a man do. I was immersed in a mundane world where the male sexual archetype was a guy who wore jeans, had big muscles, never showed his feelings, and beat up on "fags." Adam Ant was like a slap across the face— albeit from the perfumed, white, silk glove of an eighteenth-century gentleman-rogue-dandy-highwayman-prince-cowboy-Indian chief (or whatever the hell he was supposed to be)! He represented the possibility of a world in which there was a broader interpretation of male heterosexuality, in which a man could be flamboyant and still be straight, in which the romance of the past was revived.

The floodgates had opened for me, and it became clear: there was a vast world out there beyond my suburban microcosm. In this new realm chivalry abided, the beauty and pageantry of the past could rise again, and a guy like me could be the star and get the girl while wearing a ton of makeup and women's lingerie. It was a romantic world where the jocks were the jerks and the "fags" got the girls, where the rules had been redefined in our favor, where we could be dark and mysterious and sexy and complicated, where we could be heroes, where we could be . . . well, not dorks.

I was "not like the other boys," but now I could finally accept this fact. While they watched sports, I loved monster movies. While they played football, I made stop-motion films with a Super-8 camera in my basement. While they went to make bonding rituals and engaged in activities of a dubiously heterosexual nature, I was the "fag" getting all dolled up and tossing toast at my freaky friends at *The Rocky Horror Picture Show* (and, might I add, making out with future dominatrices). I was a "dork" and I knew it. And moreover, I was perfectly comfortable with the idea because I loathed all of those damn jocks and their moronic ways. I simply came to terms with the fact that while I lived in their world, I would be at odds with them.

To a teenager living in suburban America, the early '80s British music scene offered exciting new opportunities and directions. New Wave gave us a chance to be quirky and kinky; New Romantic invited us to be sexy and glamorous; Industrial constructed a dance floor on which we could vent our anger; Goth addressed the most pertinent and persistent of a teenager's emotions: sadness, loneliness, inadequacy, and feelings of isolation. In our "have a nice day 'cause everything is just peachy" society, Goth conveyed a contradictory message. Goth said, "Life is dark, life is sad, all is *not* well, and most people you meet will try to hurt you." I couldn't have agreed more.

And so one day, I left that world. At seventeen, I left home and made my way into Manhattan's Greenwich Village. The year was 1984, and New Wave/Gothic style was in full swing on the streets of New York City. I immediately knew something was different when I found tourists following me around and taking photos. I had instantly gone from being a social pariah to being the center of attention—and I liked it.

Thanks to the countless hours I had spent alone, animating in my basement, I got a job as a stop-motion animator working on TV commercials. I animated Budweiser's "Budbowl" spots for the Super Bowl (oh the irony!) as well as ads for Kellogg's, Milton Bradley, Ikea, RC Cola, Wendy's, and a host of other squeaky-clean mainstream clients, all the while remaining the "spooky guy" with the mile-high hair, gothic-horror makeup, tights, and buccaneer boots. At times, I was considered a novelty for Midwestern clients to tell their wives back home about: "And Honey, the guy who animated our little dancing donuts was a gay, Dracula-lookin' fella wearin' spooky makeup and women's tights!"

But at other times I was a dark secret to keep hidden in the cellar

The clients on this spot are born-again Christians. Quick, someone throw a sheet over that cross-dressing, Gothic animator!"

In 1988, however, MTV came a-callin'. "We are looking for something dark, spooky, and unusual," they said. The studio managers were quick to respond. "Dark? Spooky? Unusual? Boy, have we got the guy for you!" While I had been animating rather mainstream commercials for the studio, the work I had always done for myself was decidedly spooky in nature. Thus, I was hired to direct my first national spot; I would finally be able to bring my own style of gothic stop-motion to television screens across the land. The spot I came up with, "MTV Bosch," was a ten-second MTV station identification based on Hieronymus Bosch's painting *The Garden of Earthly Delights*. In it I brought to life a stop-motion version of the triptych's "Hell" panel. The piece won a handful of awards and solidified me as a young, ookie-spooky, Gothic animator/director extraordinaire, and this was a good thing—or so I thought.

I had tasted the freedom and privilege of working in one's own style, and thus it became very difficult to go back to animating football-playing beer bottles and dancing tampons. Thereafter, I stubbornly insisted on working only on commercials that were "ookie-spookie." For the next decade I found myself being really busy around Halloween, creating holiday station IDs for The Sci-Fi Channel, USA Networks, and the like; the rest of the year I spent trying to convince mainstream companies they needed flying, fire-breathing, skeletal demons in their TV commercials (and eating a lot of ramen). I found myself sending my reel out for toilet paper commercials and getting responses like, "Uh . . . as soon as we start worshipping Satan we'll give you a call."

Then, in 1994, I was walking down the street and saw an unusual sight: a girl who was decidedly Gothic. She had a mohawk of purple extensions adorned with a myriad of bones, bells, and metal trinkets. Her eyes were adorned with the thick, black, doodled-in eyeliner designs of a decade past. Her body was covered from ears to toes in a heavy, thick, black velvet dress—it was August.

I suddenly realized that I hadn't seen a Goth in ten years. Where had they all gone? Throughout the early '80s there had been plenty of places in Manhattan to go and be immersed in Gothic music. I was turned to realize that the last time I was in a room full of Goths was at Danceteria in 1984! Had Goth died? Or was I just too immured in the animation business to keep track? I cautiously approached her. "Excuse me, is there a place where people who look like us go?"

Her black lips parted, "There's a place called the Bank that has a Goth night on Fridays. Would you like to go?"

Like a dark shepherdess, she brought me back home, wayward black sheep that I was! I stepped into the club, and there before me was an amazing sight. It may have been 1994 outside, but inside it was still 1984; time had stood still for Goth, and in ten years nothing had changed. Goth was not dead. It was undead, undead, undead! And living underground.

I began to frequent the Goth clubs in New York and quickly became a local fixture. At that time Goth had a very limited and strict definition, which included wearing black all of the time, dressing in eighteenth- or nineteenth-century garb, being misanthropic, and never ever (under penalty of complete ostracism) smiling. Musically the scene had seemed to become stagnant. At these clubs, they played either Goth music from the '80s or a mix of new bands that sounded exactly like the Sisters of Mercy, replete with heavily distorted guitars, synthesizers, and drum machine rhythms. Imagine my surprise when James, a promoter friend of mine, invited me to see a performer he had booked who was a "solo acoustic Goth singer."

"Solo acoustic Goth singer?" I scoffed. "No drum machine? No electric guitars and keyboards? Will he at least be dressed like a vampire?"

Well, the performance came and went, and afterward James approached me, asking what I though of the show. "It was terrible," I replied. "I just sat through a one-hour show and I don't remember a single thing he said. I don't remember a single lyric. I am not humming any of his melodies." And in my great pomposity I continued "I put on a better show every night in my apartment!"

James called me on it. "Okay," he said, "well then, you will do your show here next Sunday night."

I had always been involved in music in one way or the other. In junior high school I sang in a band called First Degree. We played songs by Rush, Judas Priest, and the Kinks, and would throw in the occasional punk original for good measure. We mostly performed at school talent shows and small parties, and looking back, we were probably pretty awful. Still, like most teenagers brought up on (then fetal) MTV, I had aspirations of being a rock star.

When my animation career took off, I found myself working forty-eight to seventy-two hours at a time; whatever aspirations I had of becoming the sixth member of Duran Duran (and yes, I did have these dreams) fell by the wayside. Nonetheless, that didn't stop me from writing music for my own enjoyment. In the mid '90s when the stop-motion work started to dry up thanks to the growing popularity of computer animation (and to my insistence on only animating skeletons and demons), I found myself turning more to music. During this time I learned to play the acoustic guitar and continued to write songs, and I would perform them in my apartment for myself.

Still, if I told you that I did anything other than shake in my boots at James's words I would be lying. I had not performed in front of a group of people since those days in junior high school; hence, I quite literally had stomach pains and . . . ahem . . . far less than solid bowel movements for the whole week leading up to the show.

I put a great amount of thought into what I would play. At that time, I was listening to Tom Waits quite a bit (who is hardly Gothic as well as to a local, not-yet-signed band called Rasputina that was comprised of three female cellists who dressed in turn-of-the-century undergarments; consequently, much of the material that I was writing had an old-world feel to it. Given Goth's penchant for nostalgia, I didn't foresee this as being a problem. What was daunting, however, was that my songs incorporated a fair amount of black humor and satire, and comedy in any form was strictly forbidden in the world that was the Goth scene . . . so it seemed.

I knew one thing for certain: I did not want to propagate the two-dimensional cliché of the Goth performer, that is, singing about bats and spiders with hand stapled to forehead, moaning and groaning in agony about how dismal and dreary life is. So I amplified the humor by writing things to recite in between songs—little spoken word pieces and monologues that had absurd endings and led into

And then came the night of the show. It was March of 1995, on a Sunday night at Salvation (a Goth night at a small bar on Houston Street called Den of Thieves). I positioned myself on the stage before a group of fifty or so pasty-faced, dour-looking Goths. My set began with the songs "Ex-Lover's Lover" and "When You're Evil." I told my absurd little anecdotes in the interims and went on to play the tongue-in-cheek murder ballads that I had written. As the show progressed I could see a look of confusion on some of the audience members' faces as it dawned on them, "Hey, wait a minute . . . this stuff is funny?" I watched a smile begin to snake its way across the face of a girl in the front row as she bowed her head and then covered her mouth with her hand. "Must . . . not . . . smile. . . ." She silently resisted.

Then, halfway through the set, I stopped midsong and played Gothic Bingo with the audience; the winning number was of course 666. By that time everyone was grinning a wide, communal grin; they were (Goth forbid) having a good time in public! It was then and only then that my weeklong bout of chronic diarrhea began to subside.

Word about the "funny Goth performer" spread throughout the New York Goth scene, and as I booked more shows, more and more people came. Regardless, I had to start promoting. My first and natural instinct was to print up flyers. I realized, however, that at the end of a week of clubbing I would find myself returning home pockets stuffed with stacks of flyers other people had given me; these flyers would then get dumped on the kitchen counter, and most of the time I wouldn't even bother to read them. I therefore decided that I would to do something different to promote the shows.

My inspiration came from those religious tracts one gets handed on the subway. You see the cover and think, "Cool! A Bart Simpson comic book!" But by the end you realize you've been duped when you get to the scripture explaining why little Bart is going straight to hell. My version of these pamphlets was a mini comic book called "Oh My Goth!"; in them, Satan's minions would chase me as they attempted to prevent me from playing my next show (and naturally, the information for the next show would be listed on the last page). I drew, Xeroxed, stapled, and handed out hundreds of these little booklets

Oh! What a heartwarming sight it was to walk into a Goth club and see throngs of Goths sitting on the floor, reading "Oh My Goth!" and smiling (openly!) to themselves. In time, these books took on a life of their own. People would walk up to me on the street and ask when the next one was coming out! "Um, I guess a week before my next show?" I would reply.

Eventually I decided to sit down and draw a full-length version of "Oh My Goth!" and subsequently took it to the comic book publisher, Sirius, who had published my first comic book, *Chi-Chian* (a gothic, sci-fi tale about a Eurasian girl living in thirtieth-century Manhattan). I figured *Oh My Goth!* would be a shoo-in—not so. The publisher was very apprehensive about the concept of a "funny Gothic comic book"; also, their trepidation may have had something to do with the fact that the first issue of *Oh My Goth!* looked as though I had drawn it with my feet. Nonetheless, with some gentle prodding they agreed to take it on, and the comic books did rather well. Through it, I was able to open dialogue with Goths outside of New York City and around the world (or at least wherever *Oh My Goth!* was available).

Concurrently, my audience was growing, my musical career progressed, and I was signed to the premiere Gothic record label, Projekt. In 1998 they released my first CD, *The Devil's Bris*. With two Gothic comic book series on the stands, Halloween station IDs on the air, and a CD released on a Gothic record label, I had to come to terms with a simple fact: Whether I liked it or not, I had become a professional Goth!

It was no longer an issue of personal taste; Goth had become a word that would professionally define me, for better or worse. And it was all largely due to a late-night, chance encounter with an English fop on my black-and-white, twelve-inch TV screen at 4 AM, nearly twenty years prior. And he wasn't even a Goth!

I guess at that point I expected to make a handsome living creating content (comic books, CDs, etc.) for the Gothic market. I would come to learn, however, that Goth is a four-letter word in the mainstream world. Beyond seeming just downright weird and mysterious to most commercial entities, the Goth scene itself in 1998 was so small that most big businesses (major labels, toy companies, film companies, etc.) shunned it. They felt that there were simply not enough Goths in the world to merit investing in the mass production of anything. Several thousand people is a very small group to companies hoping to sell several million units of a product. As far as they were concerned, Goth equaled a dollar sign in a red circle with a line through it. Thus, countless commercial ventures conceived and pitched during that time—toys and TV pilots and such—were immediately and flatly rejected. Things seemed grim for the life of a professional Goth.

Any smart man would have moved on. Hell, I could have jumped onto the Techno/Rave bandwagon and made a mint selling glow sticks and herbal ecstasy to tens of thousands of doped-up jackasses. I would have caught them with their pants down . . . uh, literally! But the sad truth is that I was a Goth at heart and I knew it. I have, as far back as I can remember, had a deep love and appreciation for the macabre; so despite the grim financial outlook for the genre, I just went right on doing what I enjoy doing, making my spooky comics, animation, and music, and sticking up for the scene that I love.

These days I find myself flying a lot from city to city to perform my strange brand of satirical Goth music. I will often find myself sitting on an airplane engaging in a conversation with the person beside me. We exchange pleasantries and idle chitchat and eventually they ask me what I do. I tell them that I am a musician, since that seems the most relevant thing to say. "What kind of music do you play?" is always the next question, and I have to think long and hard, asking myself if I have the stamina to explain it for the thousandth time. If I'm tired, I will say that I'm a folk singer, and their (completely understandable) lack of interest will quickly lead to the end of conversation and an opportunity for me to curl up and go to sleep. But on days when I am feeling talkative and a bit feisty, the word "Goth" will come up. And then, without fail, they will ask me the inevitable question, the one that brings us here today:

"What is Goth?"

And here, in the subsequent pages of this book, is what I tell them. . . .

what is goth?

Uh . . . beats me.
Just wear some black and act like a
melancholy jackass.
That should do it.
The end.

VOLTAIRE

OR THE PURPOSES OF THIS BOOK, A GOTH IS A FAN OF GOTHIC MUSIC. GOTHIC MUSIC IS A subgenre of rock and roll that came out of the punk scene in the late 1970s. The aesthetics that accompany the Goth scene are also of equal—if not more—importance to defining a Goth. Most people who consider themselves Goths dress the part, which generally entails wearing lots of black clothing, whiteface, and black lipstick. As Goths have a great love for pageantry, fantasy, and drama, period costumes (whether taken from the distant past or distant future) are often worn as well.

Themes that appeal to Goths tend to pertain to the dark aspects of human existence—such as death, romance, and feelings of loneliness or isolation. Not so surprisingly, many Goths are drawn to the scene due to experiences of abuse, discrimination, or systematic ridicule at the hands of "normal" people (or "mundanes," as they are called in the scene).

Goths come from all walks of life. Many are teenagers who still live with their parents, but there are also many adults, even professionals such as doctors and lawyers, as well as musicians and artists. Most Goths are highly literate and creative and spend a good deal of their free time read-ing, viewing films, listening to music, or engaging in art projects.

Goths are typically not very athletic.

But there are no rigid rules and there is a lot of diversity within the scene. In fact, there are so many permutations of Gothic music and style that at times it is quite difficult to actually pin down what is or isn't "Gothic."

Nevertheless, stereotypes abound. To the mundanes, Goths are weird, black-clad freaks who are obsessed with death; they are sad *all* of the time, have no sense of humor, and are potentially homicidal. Sadly, there are those Goths who would propagate this stereotype. Take a closer look into the Goth scene, however, and you will find a rich tapestry of ideas and practices and a menagerie of colorful characters.

Oh, dear. I said, "colorful."

the many faces of goth

Here is just a cross section of some of the factions within or related to the Goth scene.

ROMANTIGOTH

By far the most recognizable group (and probably the most parodied), Romantigoths are attracted more to the "old world" aspects of the Goth scene. They favor period garb over modern clothing and may go to great lengths to recreate the romance and pageantry of centuries past.

LIKES: Candles, red wine, Gothic novels.

MUSICAL TASTES: A little of everything, but mostly "old-school" Goth.

ADVANTAGE: They dress a *lot* better than you do!

DOWNFALL: The fake English accent is a killer!

MICOL • PHOTO: JOSH RUBIN

DARENZIA • PHOTO: JOSH RUBIN

DEATHROCKER

Unlike Romantigoths, who strive for elegance, Deathrockers are more concerned with appearing freshly dug up from the grave. If a Romantigoth were a vampire, a Deathrocker would be a zombie. Their style of dress is more closely related to Goth's Punk roots and is typified by torn or distressed clothing.

LIKES: Cheap beer and horror movies—the gorier, the better.

MUSICAL TASTES: Deathrock, some Punk and old-school Goth.

ADVANTAGE: They often get cast to play Punks in movies, TV commercials, and music videos.

DOWNFALL: Punks usually want to beat them up because of it.

CYBERGOTH

More interested in the distant future than in the distant past, CyberGoths are a fairly recent addition to the Gothic family tree. They sport futuristic styles consisting of synthetic hair extensions, facial piercings, and platform boots. Unlike most of their Goth brethren, CyberGoths do *not* shy away from bright colors; they are usually big fans of Day-Glo and fluorescent makeup.

LIKES: Plastic hair, glow sticks, toy ray guns, anything that glows.

MELISSA • PHOTO: JOSH RUBIN

MUSICAL TASTES: "Oonce-oonce," throbbing, electronic music.

ADVANTAGE: They usually avoid getting beaten up by convincing the mundanes that they are Ravers.

DOWNFALL: They *are* Ravers—they just won't admit it!

RIVET-HEAD

Fans of industrial music, Rivet-heads take their name from the sounds of gears and clanging metal often sampled in the music they love. Rivet-head style centers around militaristic themes. This inclination is reflected in their music of choice, which characteristically has heavy, marching rhythms and chanted vocals; distortion is also often found augmenting the metallic cacophony.

LIKES: Found metal objects, flight jackets, military insignia.

MUSICAL TASTES: Anything that features angry German men chanting in unison over a distorted drum machine while someone kicks an oil drum with a steel-toed army boot (this happens more often than you think!).

ADVANTAGE: If you make fun of one, he'll probably kick your butt.

DOWNFALL: To actual soldiers, they seem kind of silly.

ETHERGOTH

Serene, thoughtful, and creative, EtherGoths are defined by their affinity for ambient music, Darkwave, and classically inspired Gothic music. EtherGoths are more likely to be found sipping tea, writing poetry, and listening to the Cocteau Twins than jumping up and down at a club.

LIKES: A good book, a candlelit bath, a night in with a Tim Burton movie.

MUSICAL TASTES: Ethereal, ambient, Gothic music and classical music.

ADVANTAGE: They seem a lot smarter than you.

DOWNFALL: Unless you share in their interests, you will most likely fall asleep in their company.

KAT • PHOTO: JOSH RUBIN

PUNK

Goth's progenitor and now long-lost cousin, Punk evolved from flamboyant beginnings into a series of very rigidly defined subsets. While Goths took up the mantle of drama and pageantry, present-day Punks are most often seen in working class apparel—jeans, flannel shirts, flight jackets, combat boots, and suspenders. And they are still angry as hell! Oi!

IZZY • PHOTO: VOLTAIRE

LIKES: Eating Goths for breakfast.

MUSICAL TASTES: Punk (the specific type depends on which subset you belong to).

ADVANTAGE: Punks never need to worry about their pants falling down.

DOWNFALL: Goth chicks are a lot hotter than Punk chicks!

CANDYGOTH

With yarn for hair, striped leggings, a Hello Kitty backpack, and a repertoire of stuffed animals carried around with her, she's the Raggedy Anne of the Goth world! Also known as PerkyGoths, these girls are anything but mopey and melancholy; they bounce about as though someone put a whole pack of NoDoze in their Red Devils.

LIKES: Toys, toys, and toys; Hot Topic T-shirts; and anything that is cute and spooky.

MUSICAL TASTES: SynthPop, New Wave, and bouncy '80s Goth.

ADVANTAGE: They're youthful, vibrant, and generally well liked.

DOWNFALL: You're still getting carded at age 30!

GOTH-A-BILLY

Horror meets old-school rock and roll. The Goth-a-billy owes more to Carl Perkins than to Bauhaus. Other aspects of 1950s Americana permeate the Goth-a-billy's persona, such as bowling shirts with flames, tattoos, hotrods, fuzzy dice, and gas station shirts; a Goth-a-billy will take *The Munsters* over *The Addams Family* any day. This scene is favored by manly men for whom the idea of dressing like "fruity vampires" is not an appealing one.

LIKES: Anything with flames on it, wallets with heavy chains, pinups, horror movies.

MUSICAL TASTES: Rockabilly music about zombies and the undead.

ADVANTAGE: No one will ever accuse you of being gay.

DOWNFALL: Everyone thinks you can fix their car.

THE VAMPYRE

Essentially Romantigoths with fangs, Vampyres are also attracted to the romantic, "old-world" side of Goth; the big difference, however, is that Vampyres are specifically drawn by all things vampiric. Custom-made fangs and a cape are usually requisite to being accepted by the Vampyres. Most importantly, one must have an appreciation of such vampire-related themes and be respectful of the practices and personal interpretations of the Vampyre lifestyle as seen by others in the scene.

VALERIE • PHOTO: JOSH RUBIN

LIKES: Vampire novels and movies, role-playing games, ankhs.

MUSICAL TASTES: Varies greatly.

ADVANTAGES: Countless attractive people will actually request that you bite them on the neck!

DOWNFALL: You have to be able to say, " I am 500 years old," with a straight face—and without lisping.

A Brief History of the Word

**LONG AGO IN ANCIENT EUROPE THERE EXIST-
ED A GERMANIC TRIBE CALLED THE GOTHS.
IT'S SAFE TO ASSUME THAT AT NO POINT DID
THIS RACE DON WHITEFACE AND FAKE FANGS**
or prance about performing "Grab the Bat" dances to the The
Sisters of Mercy. So, how is it that the name of this ancient people
came to describe the angst-ridden teenage vampires of today? The
answer lies beneath a convoluted tale of incongruity as people
throughout history have used, abused, and flagrantly misused the
term "Gothic" to suit their own agendas.

For the time being we shall maintain that "Gothic" means, "pertaining to the Germanic tribe, the Goths." Are you with me?

The Goths thrived throughout Northern Europe between the
third and sixth centuries, originating in what is now called Sweden
and eventually settling near the Danube River. They practiced a
form of Norse paganism and were best known for sacking, plunder-
ing, raping, and pillaging their neighbors. In A.D. 375, with the
marauding Huns hot on their heels, they took refuge within the
boundaries of the Roman Empire. They lived there in relative peace
until high taxes and other typical Roman high jinks prompted them
to rise up against their hosts.

One of the Goths' most noteworthy feats was the sacking of
Rome in the year 410. The invasion of "civilized" Rome was considered so unthinkable and savage an act that the term "Gothic"
eventually came to be used in place of the word "barbaric." For
instance, if you were to forget to wipe the vomit from your beard
after leaving the vomitorium, you might be accused of being "downright gothic!"

And so this sarcastic coupling eventually came to endow the

word "gothic" with negative attributes having little or nothing to do with the tribe of the same name. For something to be considered "gothic" it no longer had to be related or attributed directly to the Goths; it needed only to be barbaric, dark, and from outside the civilized world.

Long after the Goths had vanished into obscurity, enormous cathedrals were being erected across Europe between the twelfth and fifteenth centuries. The architectural style of this epoch was typified by the use of ribbed vaults, pointed arches, and flying buttresses. Then came the Renaissance, and with it a revived interest in the classical age. Critics of the time referred derogatorily to those grand cathedrals of the Middle Ages as "gothic"—meaning "not classical"—since these structures were not built according to the favored Greco-Roman design. The title stuck and thus "gothic architecture" got its name (posthumously!).

For centuries to come, students across the world would study "gothic architecture," edifices not built or even seen by the eyes of a single Goth. These students would soon learn that the intent of the non-Goth architects responsible for these "gothic" buildings was to create light, airy, lofty structures filled with stained glass and having a generous glass-to-wall ratio, letting in a quantity of light rivaled only by living outdoors. Their aim was to convey the ever-present light of God. So really, the "gothic" of "gothic architecture" means "bright and enlightening."

In the eighteenth century, the Age of Enlightenment helped to further vilify gothic architecture as religion was cast aside in favor of rational thought; the style became characterized as a foreboding, gloomy token of the Dark Ages. Then in the nineteenth century, under Napoleon III, the government-endorsed destruction of medieval cathedrals in France even caused several examples to be laid to waste by the public. But this all makes perfect sense when you realize that "gothic" means "bright, airy, and enlightening; dark, gloomy, and oppressive; and pertaining to a Germanic tribe known as the Goths, yet not pertaining to the Goths at all." Confused yet?

Well, too much of anything good for you will eventually bore you to death . . . hence, by the end of the eighteenth century, all of that sickeningly "enlightened" and "rational" thinking left some artists and writers with a midnight hankering for something thick, dark, and forbidden. Since the chocolate milkshake had not yet been invented, their urges had to be sated in other ways. The Romantic Movement of the nineteenth century found artists and writers abandoning reason and searching the dank crevices of all things mysterious, supernatural, and emotional in the name of exploring the darkness of the human soul. Common subjects addressed during this period were taboo sexual themes (usually played out metaphorically), bloodcurdling terror, and the unknown. And where best to have a big, bad, bloody lesbian-vampire orgy than over at the Frankenstein place, right? Accordingly, many of that time's novels were set in the dark corridors of gothic ruins; it is this choice of environment that earned the movement its name, and thus the term "Gothic literature" was born. Notable works include Mary Shelley's *Frankenstein*, the many works of Edgar Allan Poe, and Bram Stoker's *Dracula*. The honor of "first to write a gothic novel" is most commonly bestowed upon Horace Walpole for his 1764 novel, *The Castle of Otranto*, which (much to the delight of librarians, no doubt) included the subheading, "A Gothic Story."

It's an added irony that the Goths (the tribe from which Gothic literature indirectly derives its name) were primarily illiterate and had no written language at all. At least, this was the case until the end of the fourth century when the Gothic scholar Ulfilas created an alphabet just to translate the Bible. While this event was a principal catalyst in converting the Goths to Arianism (a form of Christianity), it's safe to say that it didn't help them get around to writing books about vampires. Ever.

Moving forward, in 1891 in West Orange, New Jersey, Thomas Edison invented the motion picture camera and launched the film industry. The first films focused on capturing current events, sports, and celebrities doing whatever it is that celebrities do. But early filmmakers eventually realized that they could make fictional, "acted" films. Such films included enactments of gothic novels, as their content was profoundly dramatic; Bram Stoker's *Dracula* and Mary Shelley's *Frankenstein* found their way onto the silver screen in the way of F. W. Murnau's *Nosferatu* (1923) and Edison's *Frankenstein* (1910). Other notable films of the time include *The Cabinet of Dr. Caligari* (1919) and *Faust* (1926). And thus the gothic horror flick came to be. The genre thrived and for decades to come, countless pasty-faced vampires and ghouls would parade past our movie and TV screens.

Jumping forward to the late 1970s, the Punk Rock movement—rife with anger and distrust for the establishment—was going strong in England. By 1979–1980, it had begun to fracture and evolve, splintering in various directions. While still antiestablishment in nature, some bands such as Joy Division adopted a decidedly more melancholy sound than their angry progenitors. While the punks were screaming, "We are angry that we live in this sad world," this new wave of bands was moaning, "We are sad that we live in this angry world."

Early bands of the nascent genre, such as Bauhaus and Siouxsie and the Banshees, also wore whiteface and ghoulish makeup to accent the dark overtones of their music. Most people assert that a journalist unintentionally named the scene in a review of a Bauhaus show where the band was mockingly referred to as pasty-faced, black-clad "Gothic Rockers" because of their resemblance to the vampires of early gothic horror films. But evidence suggests that the term most likely came from the manager of Joy Division as early as 1979, when he described their music as "twentieth-century, Gothic dance music." Either way, an offshoot of punk music had inherited the often misused, frequently misunderstood term "gothic," and thereafter a generation (or more) of teenagers would come to share a name with an ancient Germanic tribe they had absolutely nothing in common with.

As they say of history, it is written by the victors. Not so for the Goths, though. While they may have succeeded in crushing the Roman Empire, they never were very much liked by history. Their name has come to represent a myriad of unrelated things that were distasteful to someone, somewhere, sometime after the Renaissance.

One thing has for the most part held true, though: while the application of "gothic" has changed with each period, the underlying meaning has remained the same. The bottom line is that "gothic" equals "bad, dark, weird, and reviled by the mainstream." So really, maybe it's not such a bad name for our little musical subgenre after all.

At the end of the day, I guess it's a good thing that Rome wasn't sacked by the Normans instead of the Goths. If they had, this scene wouldn't be called "Gothic." It would be called "The Norm." It's hard enough trying to understand the twisted meaning of the word "gothic"; imagine a world where "normal" means dark, weird, mysterious, and reviled by the mainstream!

Come to think of it . . . that sounds kind of nice.

How Deep Is Your Goth?

WHAT SUMMONS PEOPLE TO THE MAGICAL, MYSTERIOUS LIFESTYLE THAT IS GOTH? THAT ALL DEPENDS ON THE INDIVIDUAL. MANY GOTHS are brought to the scene due to their perception of mainstream culture as duplicitous; they seek truth through exploring realms considered taboo by the rest of our culture. For others, it's a whole lot simpler.

The underlying philosophy of Goth is that our society is predominantly hypocritical. Goths hold that the "normal," "upstanding" members of our society who pretend to be "good" all of the time are in fact quite capable of doing evil. This is because Goths are often people who were victims of some kind of abuse—physical, verbal, or emotional—at the hands of these very same self-righteous folk.

Moreover, in mainstream culture, so much of what makes us human is denied. We are expected to be persistently happy and are discouraged from expressing any discontent or loneliness. Just tell your mom that you were sad at school today and chances are that within the week you will be sent to therapy. You'll come out of there hopped up on enough antidepressants to make a barrel of Ravers on nitrous oxide seem downright tame.

Goths know that no one can be happy all of the time; hence, they fight against this two-dimensional attitude by delving into other aspects of the human condition. Unfortunately, some Goths take rebellion a little too far by pretending that they are sad all of the time—which is, of course, just as unrealistic. This behavior is what propagates the stereotype that Goths are a bunch of humorless, suicidal mope-meisters.

For others, Goth's appeal is simply that it is a means to change the rules by which we are judged. It's difficult to draw positive attention to oneself in the "normal" world unless one is athletic, in great physical shape, and naturally attractive. But enter the Goth world, and an outcast of the "normal world" can be the most seductive Vampire, the toughest Rivet-head, or the hottest CyberGoth— simply by wearing the right corset, applying the right makeup, or conquering the dance floor. Goth, in essence, is an opportunity to turn the rules in your favor.

Goth can entail many things. For some, it represents a life-encompassing philosophy that permeates every corner of existence. For others, it is far more superficial; ask them why they are Goths and they may simply tell you, "'Cause it looks cool." Either way, whether your Goth runs deep like a dark river through your blackened heart or it just squeaks along the surface of your vinyl trousers, all who wish to be Goth are welcome!

. . . But you *will* have to dress the part. In other words, "Abandon all hope ye who enter a Goth club in khakis!"

HERE ARE MANY ARCHETYPAL LOOKS IN THE GOTH SCENE. HOWEVER, IF NOT EXECUTED WELL, YOU COULD END UP AS A WALKING STEREOTYPE. HERE ARE SOME EXAMPLES.

[*For Boys*]

SAD-SACK DRAC

The nineteenth-century noble-turned-vampire is a popular look. But finding a suitable costume that doesn't look like it was purchased from the Halloween department at K-Mart can be challenging. The only thing ancient about *this* count is the 1974 prom tux he found in his uncle's closet!

THE FESTER

Oh, the unbridled jubilation that swept through the Goth scene when balding men discovered they too could be cool if they just shaved it all off and wore long black robes!

A word of caution, though: At all costs, resist the temptation to put a light bulb in your mouth (or anywhere else for that matter).

THE GAY PIRATE

This Goth scene staple blurs the lines between buccaneer and transvestite. No one is quite sure where it came from, and as electronic music has increased in popularity, the Gay Pirate has become a thing of the past. With the overwhelming success of *Pirates of the Caribbean*, however, this look will undoubtedly be making a comeback.

Shiver me vinyl-clad timbers!

THE NAUGHTY PRIEST

This look exemplifies the devilish qualities of Gothic irony. With a drink in one hand and a cigarette in the other, this priest is lustful, lecherous, and very, very naughty. Note: This look has become less popular in recent years as it's grown increasingly difficult to compete with the real thing.

THE VAMPIRE ACCOUNTANT

You've clearly got some sense since you knew you wouldn't get very far without fangs and a cape.

But for Goth's sake—would it kill you to get some contact lenses and shave off what's left of your hair? You look like you do Nosferatu's taxes!

Perhaps you should try The Fester.

THE "MAYBE IF I GET ENOUGH EXTENSIONS AND STICK A BUNCH OF CRAP IN MY FACE NO ONE WILL NOTICE WHAT A BIG DORK I AM" LOOK

Also known as the CyberGoth look, this style has gained tremendous popularity. It's typified by loads of synthetic hair extensions and facial piercings. But for crying out loud, there are limits! Before you turn your face into a human pincushion, consider this helpful advice: If when you get out of bed in the morning you set off the metal detector at an airport in Guam, you've gone too far.

[For Girls]

THE GRAVER

Part Goth, part Raver . . . and all mixed up.

Yes, it's a great thing that 400+ Hot Topic stores can provide even rural Goths with an endless selection of counterculture accessories. But that doesn't mean you should wear them all at once!

Choose wisely—you don't want to look like a Hot Topic store exploded on you while you walked through the mall. Here's another tip: Fangs and glow sticks are *never* a good combination.

THE RENNY

While Renaissance garb can serve as appropriate attire for nostalgic Goths, you must be careful in how you pull it off. There is a fine line between an old-world Gothic maiden and a Medieval Times waitress uniform.

If you're big into Ren-fairs, go for it; but don't get pissed if someone yells, "Bar wench! A flagon of mead!"

THE CATHOLIC SCHOOLGIRL

Ah, nothing says "torturous, guilt-ridden despair" quite like Catholic school. Hence, it's no wonder that Goths love this look so much. But certainly, you must realize that there's something very wrong about a twenty-year-old girl dressing like she's eight.

Just don't act surprised that creepy old men keep hitting on you!

THE "OH CRAP, I FORGOT TO WEAR CLOTHING" LOOK

In the pursuit of Gothy garments that are lacy and romantic, some girls resort to assembling entire outfits out of lingerie from Fredericks of Hollywood. Don't fool yourself. You don't look like an eighteenth-century noble; you look like a cheap French hooker.

What am I talking about? This is a *great* look! Keep it up ladies!

THE "I'M NOT A RAVER" LOOK

Colorful Day-Glo clothes, baggy pants, platforms, glow sticks. . . . Do I really need to tell you why this is horribly wrong?

THE BLOOD SAUSAGE

Embracing aesthetics the mainstream flatly rejects, the Goth scene has long afforded ladies of generous proportions an opportunity to be beautiful and glamorous. That, however, does *not* mean that latex is your unconditional friend!

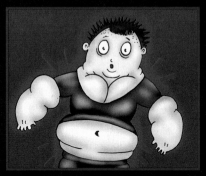

Let's keep it in perspective, ladies. Use a mirror. If you look like two hundred pounds of ground beef shoved into a rubber sock, don't leave the house. Consider flowing velvet gowns instead. You're big, you're beautiful—work it with dignity.

dude looks like the matrix!

ALK THROUGH A SHOPPING MALL IN A LONG, BLACK COAT, VINYL PANTS, AND BIG, CLUNKY BOOTS AND SOMEONE IS BOUND TO DERISIVELY yell, "Nice outfit, Neo!" The popularity of *The Matrix* has brought this particular fashion sense into the general public's consciousness; what they don't know, however, is that the ookie-spooky chicken came before the vinyl-clad egg. At least a decade before Neo started parading sci-fi noir chic through the matrix, Goth kids (particularly those of the Industrial ilk) were dressing in this style.

Underground Gothic styles have long influenced mainstream media and culture. It's continually been a blessing and a curse for Goths— while they enjoy seeing their personal aesthetics on the big screen, they simultaneously have to suffer the boorish comments of folks who don't know their counterculture history.

No matter. Goths are used to it:

(2003–1999): "NICE OUTFIT, NEO!"

(2000) "NICE OUTFIT, DARK ANGEL!"

(1999) "NICE OUTFIT, DARTH MAUL!"

(1998) "NICE OUTFIT, BLADE!"

(1997) "NICE OUTFITS, BUFFY AND SPIKE!"

(1997) "NICE OUTFIT, SPAWN!"

(1996) "NICE OUTFIT, BORG QUEEN!"

(1996) "NICE OUTFIT, CHICK FROM 'THE CRAFT!'"

(1994) "NICE OUTFIT, LESTAT!"

(1994) "NICE OUTFIT, CROW!"

(1993) "NICE OUTFIT, JACK SKELLINGTON!"

(1992) "NICE OUTFIT, DRACULA!"

(1992) "NICE OUTFIT, CATWOMAN!"

(1990) "NICE OUTFIT, EDWARD SCISSORHANDS!"

(1991) "NICE OUTFIT, UNCLE FESTER!"

(1988) "NICE OUTFIT, BEETLEJUICE!"

(1988) "NICE OUTFIT, ELVIRA!"

(1987) "NICE OUTFIT, HELLRAISER!"

(1981) "NICE OUTFIT, MAD MAX!"

(1977) "NICE OUTFIT, DARTH VADER!"

(1975) "NICE OUTFIT, FRANKENFURTER!

(1972) "NICE OUTFIT, BLACULA!"

(OKAY, SO THAT LAST ONE'S A STRETCH)

ANY PEOPLE PERCEIVE GOTHS AS ASPIRING VAMPIRES. AND YES, THERE ARE THOSE WITHIN THE GOTHIC COMMUNITY WHO DO IDENTIFY themselves as such; the majority, however, do not. While it would be fair to state that most Vampires are Goths, not all Goths are Vampires.

Rather, Vampires are Goths who have a special affinity for all things vampiric. They may dress like vampires, read vampire novels, watch vampire films, or engage in live-action vampire role-playing games; in some cities you can even find groups of like-minded vampire folk who commune to discuss topics of interest (i.e., stuff that involves vampires).

In New York City, for example, there are a handful of vampire houses, most notably, The Society Nocturnus of Gotham, the Court of Lazarus, Harlem's Hidden Shadows, and neighboring New Jersey's Court of the Iron Garden. Initiation into one of these clans is usually as simple as expressing sincere interest in being a member and abiding by the group's rules and hierarchy. Members are usually given titles and responsibilities; such duties may include ferrying messages back and forth, recording minutes at the meetings, printing flyers, or serving as an ambassador to other Vampire houses. About once a month, a court gathering is held in which the various houses convene to present their ideas, discuss their philosophies, and address their grievances. There are also elections to delegate people to various positions, such as Regent (the person who presides over the meetings). Peek into one of these meetings and you might hear a lecture on the benefits of tai chi, observe a demonstration by a renowned bat handler, or catch a performance by a local Goth band. Grievances aired may include misspelling one's illustrious title on an event flyer, wanting to oust a local fang-smith for shoddy workmanship, or anger over not being mentioned in *What Is Goth?*

In short, it's a Shriners' meeting with fangs and capes instead of fezzes.

Most Vampires are quite aware of their mortality, for while it's great fun to assume a Vampire persona and play at being immortal with friends on a Sunday night, the realities of having to go back to your job at K-Mart in the morning are all too present. Partaking in the Vampire scene in most cases is just a means of adding some much-needed romance and drama to what might otherwise be a dreary existence. In principle, it's not much different from being a fan of football: there are certain clothes you wear, certain events you attend, and certain people with whom you spend your time; the rest of your life is pretty much like everyone else's.

There are certainly those, however, who feel that drinking blood instills them with some kind of supernatural powers and who believe that they are indeed genuine vampires. This shouldn't surprise you, though; any tour of a psychiatric hospital will yield at least one Napoleon Bonaparte!

But for the most part, even the most hard-core Vampire in the Goth scene will tell you that anyone who *actually* believes they are a Vampire is just plain old nuts.

My vampiric friends
at The Court of Lazurus

CLOCKWISE: THERA, MAGDALENA, LORD AND LADY NOCTURNE, DELIRIUM TREMENS PHOTOS: VOLTAIRE

CLOCKWISE: MIKE. NAFARIOUS. 'RA UBASTI MAKING FANS FOR MIKE'. DIRE WOLF PHOTOS: VOLTAIRE

LOKI • PHOTO: MELISSA HUNT

(Or Is It the "Dramamine"?)

OTHS ARE NOTHING IF NOT MELODRAMATIC. IN ASSUMING A GOTHIC PERSONA ONE MUST BE ABLE TO PERFORM ONE'S PART WITH THE UTMOST believability. In order to do so, one must overcome a far greater challenge: erasing all trace of one's "real," commonplace life.

I mean, really, if you are going to play at being an eighteenth-century noble, having a knack for the dramatic is pretty much mandatory. It's a little difficult to pull off a séance in your mother's attic if she's constantly calling up for you to take out the trash; and when all of your friends know you as the all-powerful Count Lord Baron Malodorous, the last thing you want them to hear is, "Bernie Weinstein, you get down here this instant!" It takes real effort to maintain appearances in such a moment of crisis. One's arsenal of airs and affectations must be at the ready at all times, as even the most devastating affront to your persona can be remedied with the right reply:

"Oh, that madwoman downstairs? Yes, she seems to think I am her son, Bernard. The poor lad died a horrifyingly violent death, crushed by a wayward catapult during the Peloponnesian wars. I have taken pity on the poor, old wretch and allow her to live in my cellar."

If that doesn't work, you can always quickly staple the back of your hand to your forehead and recite "The Raven" by Edgar Allan Poe.

Then, of course, there's all of the theatrical doom and gloom. In the Gothic world, it is very attractive to be perceived as a tortured soul living in a state of unceasing anguish. Now mind you, most Goths are people who very much understand the sad state of the human condition (and may even suffer from varying degrees of depression); however, *no one* is actually as sad as one would need to be (i.e., *all of the time*) in order to be deemed über-cool in the Goth world. If you were

ly be incapable of getting out of bed or unwilling to bathe for days, much less be able to put on a cape and fake fangs and go out to a club to be "all alone" (with forty-five of your closest friends). In short, it takes a lot of work, sincerely conscious exertion, and a tirelessly brilliant performance to come across as *that* pathetic.

AMBER • PHOTO: JOSH RUBIN

Perhaps it is all of this histrionic behavior that makes Goths so keen on a different type of "drama." Enter any Goth club and you will most likely see a world—however small—of countless cliques, factions, temporary alliances, and political intrigues. You will no doubt hear whispered mutterings of who is sleeping with whom, who looks fat in her corset, how terrible the DJ's selection is, and so on. Goths plainly and simply have a penchant for drama and just can't resist the urge to gossip. A night out with Goths is kind of like *Dangerous Liaisons* in black vinyl; there is always someone trying to bed someone else who is interested in some girl who is trying to destroy you.

Moreover, all of this intrigue inevitably endows the cleverer of the Goths with a dangerously pointed wit; the less quick will acquire at least a working knowledge of sarcasm. Such sarcasm and cattiness are the characteristic sword and shield of the Goths (remember, they don't have muscles). They will wield these defenses in the direction of anyone with a pulse, Goth or not.

So, if you are going to fit in with the Gothic crowd, you will need to think like an arrogant aristocrat condescending to address the peasants around you. You will have to make sure that every comment has a negative spin on it. And if you can point to someone's most glaring fault while speaking of them, all the better. Add a British accent for extra points. Also, if you can manage it, affect a lisp and dabble in some heavy cross-dressing—nothing says "catty" like Goth, British, *and* gay!

But let's start small. See if you have what it takes to talk the talk at the most basic level of Goth conversation; recite the next part, "Last Night at the Hellfire," imagining the following scenario as you do so:

You are new to the local Goth scene. Somehow, you have managed to catch the attention of the most popular girl in the scene, and she has seen fit, in all of her graciousness, to share some of her insightful observations concerning the people around you. Listening intently with a countenance of grave seriousness is paramount. You know that if she accepts you, you will be instantly propelled to the heights of popularity within the scene; if she rejects you, you will have to go back to being a Raver.

Okay, now read the following remarks aloud. There is only one rule: crack a smile and you lose. Good luck!

Last Night at the Hellfire

- "The DJ at Hellfire sucks. He played Flock of Seagulls and they're not even Goth!"

- "Guess who works at Beauty Barn? Lady Sinestra! I went in there and she had on some dorky clothes and was wearing a nametag that said—are you ready for this?—'Kimberly!'"

- "Mistress Batty is such a whore. She's slept with every Goth guy in our scene—both of them!"

- "Oh My Goth! Did you hear about Baron Nocturne? He says he's not Goth anymore. He turned Rivet-head and now wants everyone to call him ACHTUNG-DV8-Citizen-Model-242!"

- "Last night at the Hellfire, Lady Sinestra was showing off a new top that she said she 'made' and then Mistress Batty walked in wearing the *same* top . . . which she got at the mall. *Burn!* They had a big, old catfight!"

- "Last week, Mistress Batty told Baron Nocturne he had bad fake-fang breath, so he told her she was a big, fat whore. She slapped him and one of his fangs went flying across the room! It was awesome!"

- "Get this! Lady Sinestra—hello, I mean 'Kimberly'—broke up with Baron Nocturne because he's not Goth enough for her anymore!"

- "The DJ at Hellfire sucks. He played Adam and the Ants and they're not even Goth!"

- "Holy Mother of Goth! Last night at Hellfire, Mistress Batty and Baron Noc—I mean, ACHTUNG-DV8-Citizen-whatever-his-face-is—were totally making out just to piss off Lady Sinestra! And they *hate* each other."

- "You're going to die! The DJ was playing 'Always Something There to Remind Me,' which was so apropos . . . but so totally not Goth! What is wrong with that guy?"

- "Yesterday, I was at the mall and I saw that top that Sinestra said she made—that is so pathetic—then I ran into 'YAK-DUNG-V.D.-ACHE-Kittyswing-sniffer' and he was totally hitting on me. Yuck! I hate Rivet-heads! They're not even Goth! Like, get real—I'm a dark princess of the night; I don't want to date an angry little boy. I need a man who's comfortable enough with himself to be all gay and mopey and stuff."

- "I was at Beauty Barn and I heard 'Kimberly' (a.k.a., 'Lady Syphilistra') telling someone that she was moving because the Goth scene here is lame. As if!"

- "It's official: 'Misfit Fatty' and 'YAKDUNG-V.D.-ACHE are a couple! But she told him he had to go Goth again, so now he's back to being 'Baron FrockNerdo.' I am so going to puke!"

- "I finally met the DJ at Hellfire last night. He is *soooo* cute! I asked him why he never plays any good Gothic music. Did you know Hellfire has an '80s night? I had no idea!"

- "You won't be seeing me around 'Smellfire' for a while. Last night I was dancing barefoot on the main dance floor and I stepped on a fang! I think it was Baron FrockNerdo's from, like, a week ago. It doesn't look good; it's all puffy and red and ookie. Can you get Gothic halitosis of the foot?"

goth is easy!

(Even a Monkey Can Do It!)

IT DOESN'T TAKE A ROCKET SCIENTIST TO TURN SOMETHING "GOTH," BUT IT MAY INDEED REQUIRE A BIT OF A MAD SCIENTIST. SUBMITTED for your approval below is an ordinary chimp. Follow the simple steps on the following page and watch in wide wonder as he is transformed into a Gothic monkey extraordinaire!

UN-GOTH MONKEY

STEP 1:
DYE HIS HAIR BLACK.

STEP 2:
GIVE HIM WHITE FACE, FANGS,
AND BLACK LIPSTICK.

STEP 3:
APPLY FANCY EYELINER.

STEP 4:
GET HIM A COOL HAIRCUT AND
SOME PIERCINGS.

STEP 5:
BUY HIM A NICE GOTHY OUTFIT
AT YOUR LOCAL HOT TOPIC.

STEP 6:
DON'T FORGET THE POINTY,
SKULL-BUCKLE BOOTS!

*Now give him something black and shiny to play
with and . . .
It's alive! ALIVE!

GOTH MONKEY...

... Likey the black leather banana!

what's in a name?

(Everything!)

PRIME MINISTER SQUIGGY, REVEREND HAPPYPANTS, PRESIDENT BUSH . . . WHY DO THESE NAMES MAKE US SMILE? IT'S LARGELY DUE TO THEIR IRONIC NATURE. WE EXPECT A person's name to match their persona; so, if you are dressed like an eighteenth-century vampire, it's only fitting that your name be as flamboyant and grandiose as your appearance.

Very few Goths use their given name, as it sounds far too dull. Instead, most Goths will create an alias for themselves that corresponds with their Gothic persona. The objective is generally to create a title that is dark, mysterious, sexy, and romantic, and extra points are given if it has an air of nobility.

In renaming themselves, most Goths aren't shy about plucking a moniker right out of a vampire novel or other piece of Gothic literature. On a single visit to a Goth club you are likely to meet a couple of Lestats or a handful of Vlads. Others may opt to take on the name of a notorious historical figure—like Rasputin, Anastasia, or Lady Bathory—or that of a long dead writer—such as Poe, Dante, Byron or, ahem, Voltaire.

Another commonly employed technique is to combine two words with dark connotations of their own to create a new, über-dark compound word; for instance, the ever-popular "Dark Angel" (one of the most popular names in the scene), "Raven Black," "Hell Razor," or "Eternal Darkness." Others are content to simply choose a name from the pantheon of popular Goth names like Batty, Spike, Raven, Skully, Dementia, Damian, or Deady.

The most creative souls in the scene (and the least likely to find themselves in the crosshairs of a copyright infringement debacle) will create a name completely of their own invention—like "Urkor Malravenous" or "Skulrik of the Sanguinites." These folks also enjoy the supplemental benefit of not running into someone at a club with the same name.

So, let's face it. You aren't going to make any friends at the local Goth club with a name like Bernie Weinstein. If you are going to go to the trouble of dressing in turn-of-the-century garb replete with fake fangs, cape, and walking stick, you are going to have to go the extra mile and dress your name up as well.

Use one of the techniques above to choose a new name. Or, you can create a really über-Goth name for yourself using my "Gothic Name Generator." You will need two six-sided dice. Roll the dice to pick a title from column A, a name from column B, an occupation from column C, and subjects from column D.

With any luck, you just might end up with a spiffy name like "Lord Satanus, Defiler of the Clergymen" or "Empress Demona, Defenestrater of the Bats."

Gothic Name Generator
(Male)

TITLE	NAME	OCCUPATION	SUBJECTS
2. Prince	2. Dracul	2. Impaler	2. Ravens
3. Lord	3. Lestat	3. Defiler	3. Seraphim
4. Count	4. Vlad	4. Seducer	4. Innocents
5. Baron	5. Nosferatu	5. Destroyer	5. Bats
6. Father	6. Sebastian	6. Ravager	6. Angels
7. Reverend	7. Satanus	7. Liberator	7. Virgins
8. Sir	8. Byron	8. Fornicator	8. Clergymen
9. Master	9. Diablo	9. Avenger	9. Dead
10. Duke	10. Darkness	10. Castigator	10. Crypt
11. Emperor	11. Barnabas	11. Necromancer	11. Succubae
12. Darth	12. Nocturnus	12. Defenestrater	12. Spiders

Gothic Name Generator
(Female)

TITLE	NAME	OCCUPATION	SUBJECTS
2. PRINCESS	2. ACACIA	2. SEDUCTRESS	2. NIGHT
3. LADY	3. DRACULINA	3. KEEPER	3. RAVENS
4. MADAME	4. LILITH	4. ENCHANTRESS	4. SERAPHIM
5. MOTHER	5. BATTY	5. DEFILER	5. INNOCENTS
6. COUNTESS	6. MALEFICENT	6. USURPER	6. BATS
7. MISTRESS	7. MALORA	7. VIOLATOR	7. ANGELS
8. DAME	8. LUCIDIA	8. ERADICATOR	8. VIRGINS
9. CZARINA	9. MAGDALENA	9. DECIMATOR	9. NOBLES
10. MARQUESA	10. DEMONA	10. DEFENESTRATER	10. BLACK VEIL
11. QUEEN	11. VAMPIRA	11. SCOURGE	11. SUCCUBAE
12. EMPRESS	12. NOCTURNA	12. WEBMISTRESS	12. SPIDERS

the dance of darkness

THROUGHOUT HISTORY, MAN HAS DANCED TO CELEBRATE LIFE, ENSURE A GOOD HARVEST, APPEASE THE GODS, OR ATTRACT A MATE. Well, not a lot has changed in the present. Goths may dance to celebrate those new fangs they got for Hanukkah, to ensure they get a complimentary drink ticket, or to guarantee that the door-Gods let them in for free next Saturday night. Most notably, though, one might dance to express hidden turmoil, to unleash inner demons, to liberate one's vampiric spirit like a dark whirlwind enveloping the room!

In other words . . . to hook up with girls (or be hooked up).

Nothing says, "Come back to my dark lair," (i.e., my room in Mom's attic) like a flaunting sweep of the floor with your cape.

With a dramatic wave of the arms, one successfully communicates through the dense clouds of the fog machine, "I am a half-century-old vampire."

"I shall drink of thy blood," is effortlessly proclaimed with a subtle swipe of the tongue over your fangs.

Getting kneed in the chin by an irate Rivet-head and having your fake fangs soar across the dance floor just screams . . . well . . . "I should have used Pepsodent!"

Okay—that one's a bad example.

Basically, you won't seem terribly vampiric doing the "funky chicken," and even the CyberGoths will laugh at your most immaculate rendition of the "electric slide." Do the "cabbage patch" and you will buy yourself *instant* and *permanent* banishment from the scene.

If you are going to dance the dance of darkness, you will need to do it just right. Turn the page and you will find a useful guide demonstrating just how to "pull the evil taffy," "grab the bat," and "punch the hobbit!"

Enjoy . . . and watch out for those Rivet-heads!

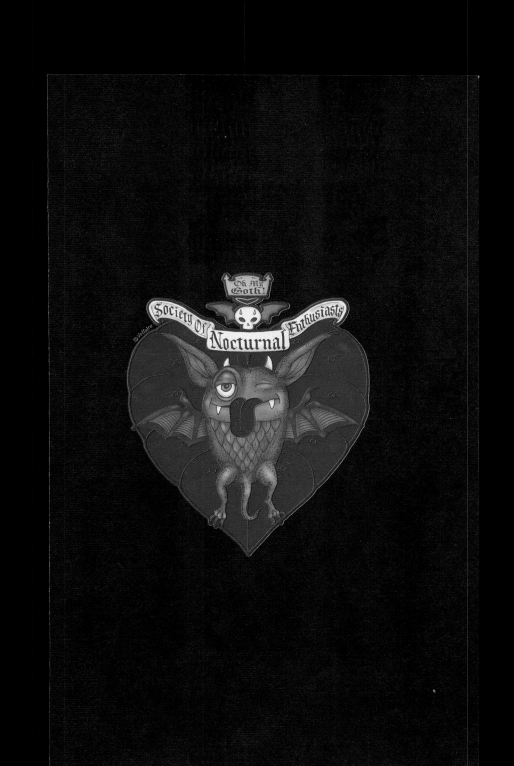

1

2

3

STAND SADLY WITH HEAD BOWED

TAKE A STEP BACK WITH LEFT FOOT

JOIN YOUR FEET AND MOPE HEAVILY

"WHO SPILLED A COKE ON THE DANCE FLOOR?"

DAVE DOES A RIVET-HEAD FAVORITE JUST FOR YOU

1   **2**   **3**

4

5

6

MOPE IN PLACE (SWAYING IS OPTIONAL)

NOW MOPE TO THE RIGHT

AND CONTEMPLATE SUICIDE

4

5

6

PIA DOES A LITTLE GOTHIC SPRING CLEANING

"MY, THIS ATTIC IS FULL OF COBWEBS!"

"I'LL REACH UP AND PULL THEM DOWN."

"AHHHHHH! A BLACK WIDOW SPIDER!"

THE GOTHIC TAI CHI DANCE
(WHOA! YOU KNOW KUNG FU?)

KAT PROVES SHE'S A BLACK BELT!

PULLING THE EVIL TAFFY
(A VARIATION ON THE COBWEB DANCE)

1

GRAB THE
EVIL
TAFFY!

2

PULL IT
TOWARDS YOUR
BLACK HEART

3

"OO. THERE'S
SOME MORE
OVER HERE!"

... AHEM... A BLACK VINYL BELT.

4

"I'M
COLLECTING ALL
OF MY ANGST !"

5

"AND FORMING
A FIERY BALL
OF CHI..."

6

"TO THROW
AT THAT
DAMN RAVER!"

1: Grab the Bat   2: Love the Bat   3: Throw the Bat Down   4: Step on the Bat

Punch The Hobbit!

Joey gets downright violent

5. Long
for
the Bat

6. Pick
the Bat
up

7. Love
the Bat

8. Let
the Bat
go!

1: ALL'S WELL WHEN SUDDENLY...

2: "MY EYE, IT BURNS!"

3: "DAMMIT, I LOST MY CONTACT LENS!"

4: "MUST SCAN THE DANCE FLOOR."

NOW GET OUT THERE AND BOOGIE!

5. "AHA, THERE IT IS!" 6. "COME TO ME..." 7. "SWEET OCULAR RELIEF!" 8. "AH, SO MUCH BETTER!"

...AND TRY NOT TO HURT ANYONE!

gothic poem generator

ANY POET-BLOUSE-WEARING DENIZEN OF A LATE-NIGHT CAFÉ WILL TELL YOU THAT THE SURE WAY INTO A SPOOKY GIRL'S . . . AHEM . . . heart is with a torturously bad Goth poem. Roll a set of dice to choose words from each column and you might end up with a dark gem like the one below.

Example:

Dark is the core of my soul.
Morbidly, I lurk through the harrowing world
until nightmares flay me of my hope.
Death, Death, Death.
Thou art my salvation.

_____ *is the core of my*_____ .
     (Adjective 1)   (noun 1)

_____ *I* _____ *through the* _____ _____
  (Adverb 1)   (Verb 1)   (adjective 2)   (noun 2)

*Until*_____ _____ *me of my* _____ .
          (noun 3)   (verb 2)   (noun 4)

_____ , _____ , _____ .
       (Noun 5)   (same noun again)   (same noun again)

Thou art my _____ .
                      (noun 6)

ADJECTIVE 1	NOUN 1	ADVERB 1	VERB 1
2. Dark	2. Soul	2. Morbidly	2. Lurk
3. Gloomy	3. Being	3. Cautiously	3. Trudge
4. Black	4. Spirit	4. Half-heartedly	4. March
5. Wretched	5. Existence	5. Sadly	5. Walk
6. Desolate	6. Consciousness	6. Unhappily	6. Do the "electric slide"
7. Pitiful	7. Underwear	7. Apprehensively	7. Crawl
8. Clammy	8. Heart	8. Melancholically	8. Creep
9. Moribund	9. Left kidney	9. Misanthropically	9. Plod
10. Waning	10. Bosom	10. Darkly	10. Lumber
11. Dilapidated	11. Cranium	11. Sheepishly	11. Stomp
12. Lugubrious	12. Nether-region	12. Creepily	12. Drag myself

ADJECTIVE 2	NOUN 2	NOUN 3	VERB 2
2. Harrowing	2. World	2. Nightmares	2. Flay
3. Frightening	3. Jungle	3. Creatures	3. Strip
4. Strange	4. Plane of existence	4. Insecurities	4. Rob
5. Horrifying	5. Reality	5. Doubts	5. Deny
6. Terrifying	6. Dreamscape	6. Trepidations	6. Rid
7. Startling	7. Land	7. Monsters	7. Remind
8. Fearsome	8. Forest	8. Childhood fears	8. Free
9. Incontinence inducing	9. Playground	9. Evil proctologists	9. Aleve
10. Scary	10. Garbage heap	10. Invisible enemies	10. Relieve
11. Ominous	11. Litter box	11. Dark shadows	11. Shred
12. Oppressive	12. Dunghill	12. Mulatto clowns	12. Purge

NOUN 4	NOUN 5	NOUN 6
2. Hope	2. Death	2. Salvation
3. Batman underwear	3. Sleep	3. Vindication
4. Fears	4. Suicide	4. Destruction
5. Dreams	5. Dreams	5. Liberation
6. Confidence	6. Demons	6. Obsession
7. Weekly enema	7. Blood	7. accountant
8. Inner demons	8. Darkness	8. Compulsion
9. Turmoil	9. Ravens	9. Demolition
10. Inner peace	10. Succubae	10. Annihilation
11. Guardian angels	11. Beetlejuice	11. Devastation
12. Dignity	12. Aunt Jemima	12. Castigation

horror poem generator

BY ROLLING A PAIR OF DICE TO CHOOSE WORDS FROM EACH COLUMN, YOU TOO CAN BECOME THE NEXT EDGAR ALLAN LOVECRAFT!

Example:

Harpies descend from the crooked trees with
Mewling infants in their gaping mouths.
The spirits call to me from beyond the grave.
Festering in the quagmire . . .
Bela Lugosi is undead, undead, undead.

_____ *descend from the* _____ *with*
    (Noun 1)   *(noun 2)*

_____ _____ *in their* _____ _____.
  (adjective 1)   *(noun 3)*   *(adjective 2)*   *(noun 4)*

The _____ *call to me from beyond the* _____.
     (noun 5)   *(place 1)*

_____ *in the* _____ *. . .*
  (Participle 1)   *(place 2)*

_____ *is* _____ *,* _____ *,* _____.
 (proper noun 1)   *(adjective 4—repeated 3 times)*

NOUN 1	NOUN 2	ADJECTIVE 1	NOUN 3
2. HARPIES	2. CASTLE RUINS	2. MEWLING	2. BABES
3. BATS	3. ROCKY CRAGS	3. SCREAMING	3. INFANTS
4. GHOSTS	4. CROOKED TREES	4. CRYING	4. VIRGINS
5. VULTURES	5. DARKENED SKIES	5. DEFECATING	5. JACK-O'-LANTERNS
6. RAVENS	6. TEAR-FILLED CLOUDS	6. YELPING	6. FLAYED KITTENS
7. SKELETAL PIGEONS	7. UNHOLY HEAVENS	7. FLAILING	7. DEAD PUPPIES
8. BLACK RUBBER CHICKENS	8. CLIFF-TOPS	8. THRASHING	8. CLERGYMEN
9. DEAD BIRDS	9. SCREAMING TREES	9. SHRIEKING	9. EVISCERATED MONKEYS
10. UNDEAD NUNS	10. HELLISH HEIGHTS	10. MOANING	10. LAB RATS
11. GHOULS	11. TOP SHELF AT WAL-MART	11. OBSCENITIES-YELLING	11. FAT SUBURBAN HOUSEWIVES
12. RUBBER BATS	12. EMPIRE STATE BUILDING	12. WILDLY GESTICULATING	12. BUNNY RABBITS

ADJECTIVE 2	NOUN 4	NOUN 5	PLACE 1
2. GAPING	2. MOUTHS	2. SOULS OF THE DAMNED	2. CRYPT
3. HORRIFYING	3. TALONS	3. FEARS OF THE LIVING	3. GRAVE
4. HUNGRY	4. LOINS	4. GHOSTS OF FALLEN SOLDIERS	4. BEYOND
5. TERRIFYING	5. CLAWS	5. CRIES OF DEAD TURTLES	5. LAND OF THE LIVING
6. MONSTROUS	6. FINGERS	6. FLAPPING OF BAT WINGS	6. TOMB
7. SINISTER	7. JAWS	7. SOUNDS OF BREAKING WIND	7. BELTWAY
8. RAVAGING	8. PINCERS	8. SHADOWS OF MY PAST	8. CONFINES OF DECENT POETRY
9. HORNY	9. CUTLERY	9. HORRORS OF JUNIOR HIGH SCHOOL	9. RIVER STYX
10. DUNG-SMEARED	10. UNDERGARMENTS	10. AROMA OF DIRTY SOCKS	10. DAWN OF THE DEAD
11. FOUL-SMELLING	11. PREHENSILE TAILS	11. SKULLS OF MY ENEMIES	11. LIMITS OF REALITY
12. CHEESE-FILLED	12. TOES	12. TENTACLES OF DOOM	12. BOUNDARIES OF BAD TASTE

PARTICIPLE 1	PLACE 2	PROPER NOUN 1	ADJECTIVE 4
2. ROTTING	2. SWAMP	2. BELA LUGOSI	2. UNDEAD
3. DECOMPOSING	3. GROUND	3. ALEISTER CROWLEY	3. UNALIVE
4. FESTERING	4. QUAGMIRE	4. ERNEST BORGNINE	4. GONE
5. FLATULATING	5. BOG	5. KAREN BLACK	5. UNDONE
6. DECAYING	6. DIRT	6. FRANKENSTEIN'S GAY UNCLE	6. DEAD
7. PUTREFYING	7. MUD	7. KING KONG'S HAIRLESS BUTT	7. NEVERMORE
8. MUMMIFYING	8. OUTHOUSE TOILET	8. DRACULA'S DAUGHTER	8. CONDEMNED
9. REGURGITATING	9. SIX FEET UNDER	9. THE GHOST OF KARLOFF	9. DEFLOWERED
10. JUGGLING CATS	10. LITTER BOX	10. THE BRIDE OF THE BEAST	10. CONSUMED
11. FEEDING THE WORMS	11. SEWERS	11. THE HOUSE OF USHER	11. VANQUISHED
12. PUSHING UP DAISIES	12. SPITTOON	12. THIS POEM	12. FORGOTTEN

ANATOMY of a RomantiGoth

FLAMBOYANT
TURN-OF-THE-CENTURY
GARB FROM YE OLDE
SHOPPING MALL

COFFIN-SHAPED PURSE
FOR CARRYING CLOVE
CIGARETTES, BLACK
EYELINER, BLACK LIPSTICK,
BLACK NAIL POLISH,
TWENTY-SEVEN GOTH CLUB
FLYERS, FAKE ID, AN
ANNE RICE PAPERBACK,
EXTRA SET OF FAKE
FANGS, AND SIXTEEN
YEARS OF
PENT-UP ANGST

ELABORATE DESIGNS OF AN ERA
LONG PAST (I.E., THE '80S)

HAUGHTY AIR OF
DARK ARISTOCRACY

GRANNY'S MISSING HEIRLOOMS

DAINTY LACE GLOVE
READY TO BE
KISSED BY A
PEASANT
(I.E., THE DJ)

BLACK
WIDOW SPIDER
TATTOO ON LEFT
ARSE CHEEK

PARASOL
TO PROTECT
AGAINST THE
EVIL, YELLOW
HURTY THING
(THOUGH MOST
OFTEN USED
AT NIGHT)

POINTY
SKULL-BUCKLE
BOOTS
(UNDER THERE
SOMEWHERE)

ANATOMY OF A DEATHROCKER

WHITEFACE, BLACK LIPSTICK, MISANTHROPIC GLARE

TOUSLED, BLACK MOHAWK, NOT TO BE CONFUSED WITH PUNK

AS MANY SKULL PENDANTS AS WILL FIT ON CHEST

MATCHING SKULL EARRING (GOTHIC BLING-BLING)

EX-GIRLFRIEND'S TORN FISHNETS PULLED OUT OF THE TRASH, RIPPED AT THE CROTCH AND PULLED OVER THE HEAD

BLACK SHIRT (WITHOUT RIPS: $20, WITH RIPS: $350, WITH ENOUGH RIPS TO LOOK LIKE YOU JUST CRAWLED OUT OF THE GRAVE: VINCENT PRICELESS

MORE BELTS THAN ARE ACTUALLY NEEDED FOR HOLDING UP PANTS

"NIGHTMARE BEFORE CHRISTMAS" BOXER SHORTS

OBLIGATORY BLACK NAIL POLISH

BIG, BLACK BOOTS FOR STOMPING OUT HAPPINESS

THE BOOTS ARE ALSO HANDY FOR KICKING THE ASSES OF GUYS WHO BELITTLE YOU (OR AT LEAST RUNNING REALLY FAST)

STRAP 1
STRAP 2
STRAP 3
STRAP 4
ZIPPER ON THE OTHER SIDE!

ANATOMY of a CYBERGOTH

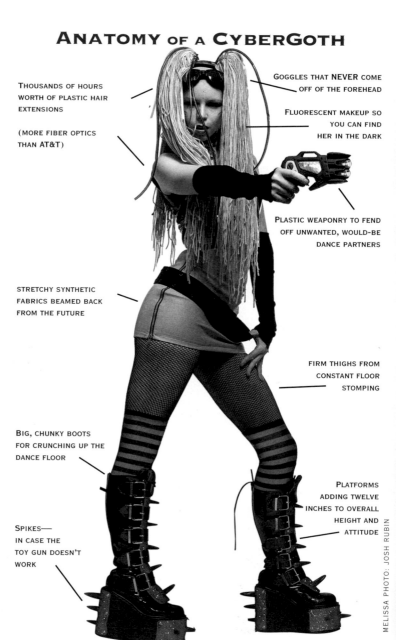

THOUSANDS OF HOURS WORTH OF PLASTIC HAIR EXTENSIONS

(MORE FIBER OPTICS THAN AT&T)

GOGGLES THAT **NEVER** COME OFF OF THE FOREHEAD

FLUORESCENT MAKEUP SO YOU CAN FIND HER IN THE DARK

PLASTIC WEAPONRY TO FEND OFF UNWANTED, WOULD-BE DANCE PARTNERS

STRETCHY SYNTHETIC FABRICS BEAMED BACK FROM THE FUTURE

FIRM THIGHS FROM CONSTANT FLOOR STOMPING

BIG, CHUNKY BOOTS FOR CRUNCHING UP THE DANCE FLOOR

PLATFORMS ADDING TWELVE INCHES TO OVERALL HEIGHT AND ATTITUDE

SPIKES— IN CASE THE TOY GUN DOESN'T WORK

MELISSA PHOTO: JOSH RUBIN

ANATOMY OF A RIVET-HEAD

THE PIERCING GAZE OF A SOLDIER LOOKING TOWARD A DARK FUTURE IN WHICH MACHINES RULE THE EARTH—JOIN IN THE CHANT! JOIN IN THE CHANT! ANARCHISTS UNITE!

COPIOUS QUANTITIES OF EXPOSED SCALP FOR BETTER AERODYNAMICS

MULTIPLE PIERCINGS TO BETTER ACCOMMODATE THE CYBERNETIC IMPLANTS WE WILL SURELY BE GIVEN BY OUR EFFICIENT, GERMAN ROBOT MASTERS

FLIGHT JACKET (HEY WAIT A MINUTE, THAT'S NOT A FLIGHT JACKET! THIS IS ONE SHARP DRESSED RIVET-HEAD!)

THERE'S A FRONT 242 T-SHIRT IN THERE SOMEWHERE, TRUST ME!

CLENCHED RIGHT FIST FOR PUNCHING THAT COMMUNIST HIPPIE SCUM ON THE DANCE FLOOR ACCIDENTALLY/ON PURPOSE

CLENCHED LEFT FIST FOR PUNCHING THAT CAPITALIST YUPPIE SCUM ON THE DANCE FLOOR ACCIDENTALLY/ON PURPOSE

COMBAT BOOTS FOR FERVENTLY MARCHING OUT AGGRESSION ON THE STICKY DANCE FLOOR OF SONIC OBEDIENCE (WHATEVER THAT MEANS)

THIS THING IS GOING TO COME IN HANDY WHEN IT'S TIME FOR OUR ROBOT MASTERS TO TIE US UP FOR THE NIGHT

LOTS OF LOOSE METAL BITS TO ADD TO THE METALLIC CACOPHONY EMANATING FROM THE SOUND SYSTEM

ALEX • PHOTO: JOSH RUBIN

57

gothic makeover

EING THE BELLE OF THE BALL AT THE LOCAL GOTH CLUB CAN BE AS SIMPLE AS PUTTING ON the right makeup. In fact, it's as easy as 1, 2, 3—or in the case of our Gothic makeover demonstration, 1, 2, 3, 4, 5, 6, 7, 8, 9, 10, 11, 12, 13.

Watch in horror and awe as makeup artist extraordinaire Amelia Preston (not a very spooky name; maybe she should use the Gothic Name Generator on pages 38–39 turns our hapless, doe-ish victim into a veritable queen of the night!

1. Aww! Isn't she sweet and innocent? Not for long . . . Mwahahahaha!

2. Amelia explains the process to Audrey (i.e., warns her of the impending transformation).

3. Foundation is applied. Make sure it's no more than three shades lighter than your natural skin tone; we're creating a Goth, not a circus clown.

4. Be sure to blend below the chin line (unless you want to look like an evil mime).

5. Powder is used to give a nice, matte, pale, just-risen-from-the-grave pallor.

6. White pearlescent powder is applied to the brow bone to bring out the eyes.

7. Ah, the obligatory black eyeliner! Use pencil for the bottom, liquid for the lid.

8. Apply eye shadow to the lids. Use a medium base color—like blood red, ghoulish gray or monstrous magenta (don't bother looking for these colors; we made them up!).

9. Curl your eyelashes and apply mascara; they will need to be extra long if you're going to catch flies with them like Aeon Flux. It helps if you have a picture of a skull next to your head.

10. Ah, the obligatory black lipstick! Line the lips with black pencil first (an eyeliner pencil will do just fine).

11. Fill in the lips with a brush coated in black lipstick.

12. Moisten a small-angle brush, swipe across a black eye shadow and use to define the eyebrows for that "eyes of the midnight jungle" look.

13. Go out and get yourself a nice Gothy haircut, have your photo taken next to a candelabra and now you are ready to take the Goth scene by storm!

14. **EXTRA CREDIT:** Spend an additional fifteen minutes with liquid liner to further embellish your brows and eyes with ornate designs for the *ultimate* über-Goth look.

Siouxsie Sioux would be proud!

. . . and remember, Mom, under all of that wacky makeup she's still your daughter!

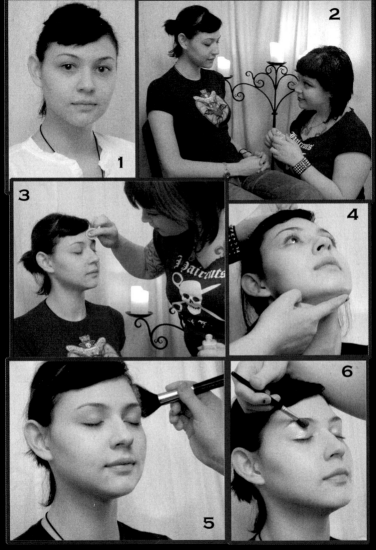

59

12

13

14

cybergoth hair makeover

BEHOLD OUR MODEL, ANGELICKA. OH SURE, SHE'S GOTHY ENOUGH—BUT WE CAN REBUILD HER, MAKE HER STRONGER, FASTER, MORE CYBER THAN EVER BEFORE!

1. CyberGoths, start your engines!
2. Lana parts Angelicka's hair and begins adding black synthetic hair extensions.
3. Each extension is braided into the natural hair and held in place by tiny, black rubber bands.
4. The individual strands are teased with a comb (Nya-nya nya-nya nyah nyah!) for that matted-dread look.
5. A wig steamer is then used to melt the hair into place.
6. Three down, several dozen to go.
7. Brightly colored strands of synthetic hair (in this case, electric blue) are added to the mix.
8. I don't know how much more of this I can take!
9. Six hours later, Angelicka has extensions on half of her head.
10. Eleven hours later, all of the extensions are in, and the patient Angelicka hasn't killed anyone yet.
11. The hair is tied up by knotting it and using rubber bands to hold it in place.
12. The bangs are trimmed.
13. Angelicka from behind. Doesn't it look nice?
14. Oh my God! What's that maniac doing? Heh heh heh. All of that extraneous hair is removed with electric clippers.
15. The back and sides of the head are shaved clean.
16. Voila! A CyberGoth is born. She's beautiful, she's lovely . . . and if you get too close to her on the dance floor, she will *stomp* on you!

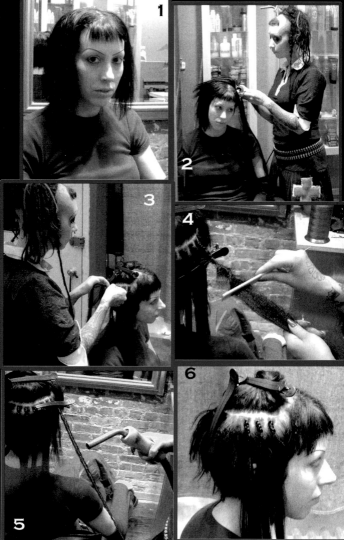

HAIR NURSE LANA PHOTO: VOLTAIRE

Skulls

Goths love skulls. Mundanes have an
irrational fear of them.
Four hundred years ago, if you saw a
big black flag with a skull on it in the
Caribbean, you had reason to worry.
It meant you were probably going to be
killed, robbed, and/or raped—
not necessarily in that order.
Nowadays, if you see a guy in a black
T-shirt with a skull on it all that means is
that he probably lives near
a mall that has a Hot Topic
store in it.

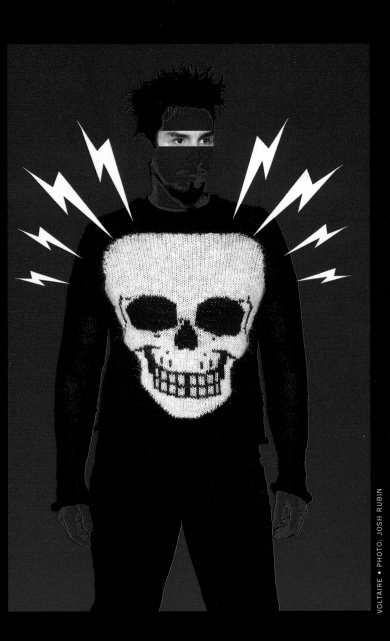

my skull sweater

—a matter of national security

AFTER 9/11/2001, THINGS CHANGED PRETTY DRASTICALLY IN THE WORLD OF AIR TRAVEL. THROUGHOUT THE UNITED STATES WE ALL BECAME a little more accommodating when it came to the question of security. Even New Yorkers—a hardened lot if there ever was one—would pop off their shoes, take off their belts, and accept the inconvenience with a smile, knowing that it was all in the name of keeping our country safe.

As a touring musician, I often find myself walking through airports with my guitar slung over my shoulder. I have a favorite hand-knit sweater that I often wear when flying; it's black with an enormous, white, angora skull on the front. Immersed as I am in the world of all that is ookie-spooky, I am admittedly rather desensitized to what might be perceived as macabre imagery and relatively oblivious to the stir my appearance might occasionally cause. And so on countless trips, in my skull sweater, I have endured the lengthy lines at security, the X-raying of baggage, the taking off of shoes, simply doing my civic duty as an American, patiently, politely—nay, even proudly.

Ah, shoes . . . it's at this point that I am compelled to pause and tip my hat to that would-be-successful terrorist, Richard Reid. Trouble was afoot on American Airlines, Flight No. 63, when this heel—explosives embedded in his sneakers—tried to execute a preposterously cartoonish attempt to blow up the plane by setting his shoelaces on fire. In doing so, he touched the lives of oh so many millions of travelers and added some extra inconvenience to our already irksome lives.

It's little consolation that he will spend a good portion (if not all) of his life behind bars; certainly his crime deserves a more fitting punishment—like having a certain desert bird "beep-beep" an enormous Acme anvil on him from a great height. Still, I suppose we should all be grateful that he didn't hide the explosives in his rectum! Yes. This and so many other such pleasant thoughts have filled my head while standing complacently in my skull-adorned socks (to match the sweater, of course) in those lengthy lines at airport security.

But then came the random searches.

Oh, they didn't seem so bad at first when the plan was to pull aside travelers completely at random. Sure, searching an eighty-year-old woman seemed a little pointless, but then you never know. Terrorists are everywhere, and they could be anyone; even the man standing next to you could be a terrorist! It was only prudent that there should be random searches. We were all getting the point—it was for our own good.

Hell, if an atomic bomb had gone off right then, I would have probably run around looking for a 1950s school desk to duck under. I was sold.

Time and time again, I gleefully submitted myself to the random searches. That is, until I realized that I was being "randomly" searched on every flight. Could I really be that lucky? Or was it something else?

I got to thinking about all of those flights, and I concluded that there was nothing random at all about the selection process. There was a pattern, and it seemed to go like this:

First, they would pull over an eighty-year-old Jewish grandmother. *Who* is this woman a danger to?!? Granted, matzo balls may be similar in shape, texture, and occasionally taste to plastique; still, I think it's safe to say that the old yenta with the schvata on her head is a danger to no one—that is, unless she sits next to you and chews your ear off about how her son, the dentist, never calls her.

Then they would pull aside the chubby American family—the chubby mom, the chubby dad, and their two-and-a-half chubby kids.

The law of averages dictates that the family chosen will be chubby since 61 percent of Americans have a "glandular problem"—and/or love donuts. The fact that they look so innocuous really adds to the seeming randomness of it all. But, truth be told, the only person who need fear this family is the owner of the all-you-can-eat buffet.

After they'd set the "oh dear, isn't this all so terribly random" tone, they would then pull aside the dark-skinned fellow in the turban. If there were no dark-skinned fellow in a turban on that particular flight, then any ol' brotha' would do.

And lastly, you guessed it . . .

The monologue goes something like this: "Hey y'all, we're gonna be searchin' some people at random here. Alright, we got the little old lady. Good. You, chubby family, can you come with me, please? We need two more. Let's see . . . two more people . . . totally random now . . . okay. How about the Negro and the evil hippy in the skull sweater?"

Over the course of this little tale, you should have arrived at two conclusions about me. First, I am very long-winded—I think that's clear. Second, I am not very bright, as the big revelation in respect to all of this came to me completely by accident.

Let me begin by saying that usually, after a performance, I like to enjoy the spoils of war, so to speak. I will do a little meeting and greeting, have a drink, dance, and engage in all matter of frivolity until they kick me out of the club. Eventually, I go back to the hotel, and late the next afternoon I get on a plane, get randomly searched, and go home to New York City.

Well, after a particular show, the promoter foolishly booked my return flight at the crack of dawn. Consequently, after consuming my fair share of liquid revelry, I headed straight for the airport. I hadn't had time to change into my comfy, huggably spooky skull sweater, so I went in the black Jean Paul Gaultier suit I was wearing at my show.

I first noticed that something was horribly wrong when I was checking my baggage and they didn't ask me to haul it over to the X-ray machine; they just dropped it onto the conveyor belt and off it went to the plane. Then I arrived at security. I was met with choruses of, "Hello Mr. Voltaire! Can we carry your bags, Mr. Voltaire? Can we please upgrade you to first class, Mr. Voltaire?" I was stunned. I began to wonder what I had done to deserve such treatment; I tried to figure out what was different about this time.

And then it hit me—I wasn't wearing my skull sweater!

Could it really be that simple? Could people really be that stupid? I decided to test out this theory. So, on the dozens of trips I have taken since that moment, I have worn a suit to the airport each time and have yet to be randomly searched. Apparently a musician wearing a big skull on his chest is a degenerate and a danger to society. A musician wearing a suit is something else entirely—a rock star.

Now I wear my skull sweater where I know it won't cause me any inconvenience. And yet, sometimes I'm still surprised.

At one point, while walking down St. Mark's Place in New York City's East Village (if there were ever an accepting and progressive place on Earth it's there) I was stopped by a Ukrainian woman. "You are Christian?" she asked me.

I was befuddled. "Uh, no," I responded.

"You are Satanist?" she continued in a thick accent.

Now I was really confused—is that the only other option if you're not Christian? "No! No, of course I'm not a Satanist!"

"Then why you have this skull on chest?" she pressed.

"A skull is *not* Satanic!" I answered.

"Yes! This is Satanist! This is Satanist!" and now she was wildly gesticulating.

"Calm down, lady," I rebutted. "The Devil did not make your skull. *God* made your skull to protect your puny, judgmental brain!"

SINCE THE DAWN OF TIME, MAN HAS FEARED THE UNKNOWN. WHILE MOST OF MANKIND REGARDS THE EXPANSE OF UNCERTAINTY AS A dark and mysterious cauldron of dreadful possibilities, there have always been those few individuals who embrace it. To these brave and adventurous souls, it entails a chance to experience something new, to glance into an exotic world, or to change what is staid in our daily lives.

In this spirit, Goths venture forward into this hallowed territory. They gaze into the shadows of the forbidden and look intently upon the human soul to see what lurks there in the darkness. They mine these depths for new experiences, for a new awareness, or more often than not just for some spooky fashion tips. Naturally, they wear these newfound perspectives on their sleeves as badges of honor, manifested in the way of velvet capes, vinyl corsets, and patent leather boots. They assume the appearance of "the unknown" and are therefore feared and shunned by the teeming masses of "mundanes"—those who don't dare to look into the pit of their own souls for fear of what they might find.

The truth of the matter is that everyone is evil.

And everyone is good.

In varying degrees, we all are a mixture of the two. In our two-dimensional society, however, everyone is expected to be unrealistically good all of the time; still, we all secretly know that hidden deep inside (and in most cases, not so hidden) lurk dark thoughts, murderous urges, and taboo fantasies. Most reasonable people understand that the mere existence of such fleeting notions does not necessarily warrant actualizing them. Goths recognize this fact and are comfortable with the notion of selecting which of these fantasies are appropriate to enact.

For instance, that urge to hook up with the two scantily clad Goth chicks at the end of the bar might seem worth pursuing. Whereas, the desire to hack your ex-lover's new lover up into tiny little pieces and mail him to a P.O. Box in Guadalajara would best be left as a delicious fantasy to enjoy in the privacy of your own mind.

Not everyone, though, is comfortable with the idea of evil notions flitting through their minds, even if only for an instant. It seems that many mundanes fear these feelings and spend most of their time trying to keep them hidden from the rest of the world; daily, they fight an internal battle to deny the existence of these less-than-pure thoughts. Hence, when a Goth appears before them, that Goth becomes the incarnation of their fears, a manifestation of their own insecurities, a symbol of the frightening unknown. They lash out violently—verbally and/or physically——as though by attacking the dark creature before them they are somehow wrangling the inner demons against which they are so helpless. The ongoing war within spills out onto an external battlefield; here, the enemy is no longer themselves but a scapegoat dressed in the colors of their darkest inner strife.

Then again, maybe they just hate us 'cause we look funny.

Either way, a Goth gets his butt whooped for nothin'!

Yes, yes, I know that I dress like a vampire. What's that? Yes, I know that vampires don't exist. Come again? Why do I dress like a vampire even though I am not one? Probably for the same reason that you wear a baseball uniform even though you're not on a baseball team.

VERYONE! AS THEY ARE GENERALLY MISAN-THROPIC, ONE COULD SAY THAT GOTHS HATE ALL OF HUMANITY—INCLUDING THEMSELVES. THIS would be a really gross generalization, however, as well as just highly impractical. In day-to-day life, there are lots of people who Goths encounter, and honestly, it would require far too much energy to hate them all.

Naturally there are going to be people Goths hate less than others, just as there are certainly those who are more deserving of their hate. At the top of the hate list would be people who go out of their way to poke fun at, mock, ridicule, or condemn Goths. These people tend to be the rather mainstream folk who don't care for—or perhaps are afraid of—any deviation from the norm. They often include jocks (note: an analysis of why being athletic would make you prone to disliking individuality and nonconformity is too lengthy an investigation for the limited pages of this book). Other common antagonists of Goths are those who see themselves as religious and who perhaps feel they have a set of dogma to follow and, apparently, to impose on others.

The truth is, however, that Goths tend to get along swimmingly with just about anyone who accepts them as they are. Goths are particularly accepting of anyone whom they identify as a peer. Enter a Goth club in a polo shirt and khakis and you will be regarded as a possible foe, there to poke fun at them. But enter in black clothes—of any style—and you will be warmly received. Moreover, no strangers to discrimination, Goths are usually very accepting of all races, creeds, faiths, sexual orientations, and lifestyles as long as they get a fair amount of reciprocity.

If you already are a Goth, other Goths will welcome you with open arms. At least until they get to know you . . . then the *drama* begins.

Halloween Pie

Americans love pie. Some more than others. Some people eat pie every day,
regardless of whether it's good or bad for
them. Goths are people who like
Halloween—a lot. They like Halloween as
much as you like pie. If you don't like
Goths, don't get your knickers all in a
twist. Going out of your way to ridicule
them just takes up valuable time. Time
you could be spending . . . eating pie.

Goths are harmless.

Just give them some candy corn;

they'll go away.

HE GOTH SCENE AND THE MUNDANE WORLD HAVE ALWAYS BEEN AT ODDS. THIS RIFT IS LARGE-LY DUE TO A MINISCULE BREAKDOWN IN communication resulting simply from the misapplication of certain words.

For instance, the mainstream associates the word "spooky" with things that illicit fear, and consequently the word has negative connotations. Truth be told, if Goths spent a lot of time around real spiders, skulls, and bats, they too might feel this way. The spiders, skulls, and bats that actually pervade the lives of most Goths come in the way of T-shirt designs, stickers, tattoos, and that sort of thing; they are only representations of those potentially harmful things—and are thus, in and unto themselves, completely harmless. Goths understand this; the mainstream does not. Mundanes seem to have an irrational fear of such imagery. It's as though they believe that the bats painted on the back of a DeathRocker's leather jacket might come to life and fly about the mall biting people at random. As *awesome* as that would be, it's never going to happen.

To Goths, "spooky" is a term that, for the most part, refers to an aesthetic. Black, pointy, patent leather boots are "spooky" because they invoke the image of a dominatrix-witch flying over nineteenth-century London on a broomstick. A coffin-shaped lunchbox is "spooky"—as is anything with a skull on it—because Goths have a love affair with the romantic depiction of death; this is not to say that Goths want anything to do with the real thing.

Here is another prime example: I wear a sweater with a huge skull on the front and like to come across as the big, bad, evil guy—but show me that glue trap in the kitchen with the half-dead, wriggling mouse on it and you will hear me shriek in terror like a three-year-old baby girl!

The mundane world is a place that endeavors to maintain a bright, cheery, and optimistic appearance. Just under the surface, however, there are truly dark and very real forces at play that put to name anything a Goth could come up with. There is nothing "spooky" about the denizens of the "normal" world; however their phony, perky happiness (induced by drowning themselves in antidepressants), their insidious duplicity, and their holier-than-thou self-righteous stances are nothing short of "creepy."

Unlike "spooky" things—which look cool but are essentially innocuous—"creepy" things are all too real and more often than not come in disguise, hiding in the "normal" world of the mundane, where they thrive. "Spooky" is dark, mysterious, sexy, and cool (and largely based on the fictitious), while "creepy" is that very real feeling you get when you are putting money into the offering bowl at church and suddenly notice that huge diamond ring on the pastor's finger. Think about it: you are far more likely to encounter a scheming televangelist, crooked politician, or even mass murderer than you are to come across a vampire, ghost, or flesh-eating zombie.

Nevertheless, most mundanes have a fear and loathing of all things "spooky," while seeming perfectly content to live in an almost perpetual state of creepiness. While David Lynch seems to get it—and has made a rather successful career out of exposing the creepiness of the "normal" world—it's all very confusing to us Goths. For while Goths wear their spookiness on the outside and are largely harmless on the inside, mundanes keep their creepiness hidden, employing their socially acceptable pretenses as a disguise. Their world is populated by "respectable" CEOs who pay themselves millions while laying off thousands and embezzling the pensions of their employees; "spiritual" people who go to church every Sunday but live lives full of hate and bigotry; "divinely appointed" televangelists who bilk millions from well-meaning, gullible people and subsequently spend it on their own luxurious lifestyles; "pro-life" activists who kill doctors; countless "upstanding" corporations that knowingly kill our planet to save an extra cent on the dollar; and (the very worst one of them all) the eighty-year-old lady who gives you nasty looks for having funny hair even though hers is bright blue . . . for Pete's sake!! Goths may have a quirky fascination with "spooky" things, but these things pale in comparison with the "creepy" world of the mundanes.

Once you come to understand the difference between "spooky"

and "creepy" you will most likely realize an interesting fact: "Spooky" Goths are essentially bad on the outside and good on the inside, while many "creepy" mundanes are good on the outside and bad on the inside.

In case you are still not clear on the difference between "spooky" and "creepy," here are some other helpful examples:

Goth Is "Spooky"— Normal Is "Creepy"

Wearing black all of the time is spooky.

Wearing any other color all of the time is creepy.

(Think about it—all purple?)

Impersonating a vampire is spooky.

Impersonating a police officer is creepy.

Elvira was spooky.

Elvis was creepy (at least toward the end there).

Wearing women's fishnets over your clothes is spooky.

Wearing women's fishnets under your business suit is creepy.

Putting on whiteface is spooky.

Putting on blackface is creepy (especially if you're the white governor of a southern state).

Having twenty-seven skull T-shirts in your closet is spooky.

Having twenty-seven skulls buried in the crawl space under your house is creepy.

Being hated by everyone around you is spooky.

Hating them all back is creepy (but completely understandable)!

Freaking out your parents is spooky (and an age-old human tradition that people seem to forget about once they become parents).

Calling your child a freak is creepy (and really counterproductive).

WWE

As long as millions of Americans are tuning in to see grown men in spandex hot pants breaking metal chairs over each other's heads, I should never have to be ashamed of dressing like a vampire and going to a dance club with my friends.

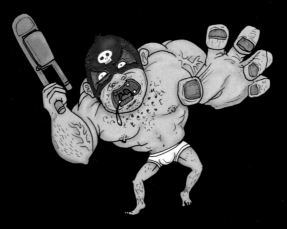

The Sad Truth About Goth

Most people think that Goths are volatile freaks obsessed with death and gore. Don't be fooled. They're basically just melancholy, more likely to commit suicide than homicide. And for that matter, they aren't really sad all of the time; this is primarily just an act that empowers them with an air of mystery. The truth is that very few Goths actually kill themselves—they'd much rather contemplate suicide and then just write a really bad poem about it.

LOKI • PHOTO: RACHEL EURYDICE

politics

MOST GOTHS ARE MORE CONCERNED WITH WHO IS SPINNING AT THE LOCAL CLUB THAN THEY ARE WITH WHO IS RUNNING IN THE NEXT presidential election. Goths share very little in the way of a communal political view, contrary to the mainstream's fears that Goths are amassing across the land consciously plotting the end of civilization as we know it. The truth is that the Goth scene is divided by too many opposing viewpoints for something like that to ever happen; there are right-wing Goths and left wing Goths—but most are just plain old bat-wing Goths who have little to no political affiliations at all.

Given all of the diversity in the scene, it's hard enough getting a group of Goths to join forces long enough to throw a party, let alone start one! Of course this is not true of all Goths; there are those who are very interested in civil affairs. On occasion, groups of Goths have been known to collaborate on humanitarian efforts, such as donating toys to the Toys for Tots campaign, putting together fund-raising concerts that benefit a charitable organization, or even organizing a blood drive (vampires giving blood—it's a sight that is truly not to be missed).

In short, one need not worry about a dark, third party rising through the ranks of the electoral process. At the end of the day, the average Goth's idea of "politics" can be summed up with this phrase: "Who do I have to suck up to to get on the guest list?"

Sheep in Wolf's Clothing

Don't worry about the guy in the black lipstick. He won't do you any harm. How is his dying his hair going to affect your life? People who go out of their way to call attention to themselves through their appearances have little to hide. No one is ever going to try to blow up a plane dressed as a vampire. No one is ever going to break into your home disguised as a mummy.

If you feel the need to be anxious about the people around you, worry about the senator in the business suit who spent your hard-earned tax dollars on an "Interns Gone Wild" cruise to Cucamonga.

(Goth or Not Goth?)

**EY, WANT TO SEE A BUNCH OF GOTHS RIP-
PING EACH OTHER TO SHREDS? IT'S EASY. GO ON-
LINE, LOG ONTO A GOTHIC CHAT SITE AND TYPE**
in this phrase: "Marilyn Manson is my favorite Goth band." The
unbridled verbal hostility that will ensue will be enough to keep
you in stitches for hours. You will be called names you never knew
existed by hordes of Goths incensed at your obvious lack of Gothic
musical knowledge. Then you will witness throngs of other Goths
come to Marilyn Manson's defense.

The "Marilyn Manson: Goth or not Goth?" question has been a
hot button in the scene for years. Why? It's mostly due to the fact
that the man and his music are popular. And "popular" to Goths
means "bad." Goth has always been underground. The appeal of the
Goth scene can largely be attributed to its obscurity; this aspect
infuses the scene with an air of mystery.

Truth be told, it's a special person who is drawn to the scene—
especially when you consider the amount of abuse they will endure
from the world around them for doing so. That being said, picture
this:

Along comes Marilyn Manson styling himself in decidedly
Gothic aesthetics. He sells millions of records and thus inspires
hordes of teenage fans to emulate his appearance. Suddenly, there
are teeming masses of kids who are perceived as "Goth" who never
even heard of Bauhaus or Siouxsie and the Banshees. Suddenly, old-
school Goths find themselves described as "one of those Marilyn
Manson fans." And nothing gets an old-school Goth's black hair dye
boiling quite like being compared to a "Mansonite."

While Manson owes more to Alice Cooper than he does to Peter
Murphy, he has undoubtedly succeeded in bringing the Gothic aesthetic to a mainstream audience (an accomplishment rivaled only by
the cinematic contributions of Tim Burton). And for this he should

be congratulated! Moreover, whether they like his music or not, Goths should be thankful for so eloquent a spokesman as Manson. Every time some black-clad kid has committed a major no-no, Manson has suffered the slings and arrows on behalf of an entire community that for the most part disavows him, and he has consistently done so with intelligence and dignity.

So, maybe his music is rather commercial. And perhaps it leans more toward Heavy Metal than Goth. But seeing as how these days a damn Raver, jumping up and down to what can only be described as "Techno in disguise," can be considered a Goth, who's to say that Marilyn Manson can't.

Either way, it's doubtful that he's moping all the way to the bank.

WELL, HERE WE ARE AT THE MELANCHOLY END OF WHAT IS GOTH? IT IS WITH A HEAVY (ULTRA-FLAT BLACK) HEART THAT I BID YOU ALL A FOND ADIEU.

If you are a visiting denizen from the mundane world, I hope you have learned something about this fascinating subculture that I call home. If you count yourself among the growing throngs of Goths in the world, I hope that I was able to part your black-lined lips into a rare smile and bring a fleeting ray of light into your otherwise gloomy existence. Either way, I hope you have found your stay here at least entertaining, if not educational. For whatever it's worth, you now know all that I do about Goth—which is quite a bit, and at the same time absolutely nothing.

While Goth once had a very fixed set of parameters ("Must wear black! Must be spooky! Must not smile!"), it has evolved from its humble beginnings to such a degree that I sometimes hardly even recognize it. The scene has been taken in countless directions by all of those intrepid individuals out there who were drawn to it by one aspect or another; these people have taken Goth under their leathery wings and added their own spin on the genre. The big '80s umbrella that was Gothic/New Wave/Industrial has espoused a colorful (Eek! There I go saying "colorful" again!) brood of offspring—including EtherGoth, Darkwave, Apocalyptic Folk, EBMGoth, ElectroGoth, CyberGoth, Orchestral Gothic Metal, GothPop, CandyGoth, PerkyGoth, Goth-a-billy, Zombie Rock, ProgGoth, GlamGoth, GangstaGoth (I just made that last one up. Heh heh!) . . . the list goes on and on.

The new permutations Goth will assume are countless and lie in the imaginations and idiosyncrasies of those brave souls willing to stand up and say, "I am a Goth," despite the ridicule they will

Or will they?

The rest of the world seems to be catching on. Big business has even come to recognize the buying-power of this growing scene. As I write this note, the shelves at comic book stores everywhere are being filled with a growing list of Goth-specific toys: The Living Dead Dolls, Bleeding Edge Goths, Kinder Goths, and Tim Burton's Tragic Toys, to name just a few. Slave Labor, Sirius, and Vertigo keep pumping out the Gothic comic books.

Hot Topic—known for (among many things) carrying Gothic merchandise and apparel—has grown to a whopping five hundred-plus stores throughout malls across America. Mighty Fine's adorable Goth chicky, Ruby Gloom, is on everything from shirts to coin purses. And for crying out loud, you can't swing a dead cat without hitting something that has Emily Strange printed on it somewhere! Projekt, Cleopatra, and Metropolis continue to keep American Gothic music alive. Moreover, Goth has found its way onto Top 40 radio with the dark stylings of Evanescence (visually at least, if not musically), and even Hollywood has seemed to go Gothic crazy with the gothic-sci-fi chic of *The Matrix*, the RomantiGoth-meets-Fetish look of *Underworld,* and obviously in the straightforward titling of *Gothika*. For Goth's sake, there's even a trivia game out there called "Goth"!

So what might mainstream acceptance portend for Goth (a scene whose very appeal lies in its back-alley, underground mystique)? Only time will tell.

My guess is that it could become mainstream for a while and then, after a few years of being in the spotlight, will revert to that dark, elusive, slimy thing you find under a rock—what it has been since after its heyday in the '80s. And when that time comes, should you look under that rock, I will probably still be there.

So, feel free to stop by for a clove cigarette and glass of red wine. You can then remind me that once, long ago, you read my book. You will ask me, "What is Goth?" and I will tell you, "Uh, beats me. Just wear a lot of black and act like a melancholy jackass. That should about do it."

You will give me a disapproving look, and I will straighten up and say, "Okay, you tell me. What is Goth?"

And you will give me the correct answer:

"It's whatever you want it to be."

OTHER WORKS BY VOLTAIRE

Chi-Chian comic book mini-series issues 1–6

Oh My Goth! comic book mini-series issues 1–4

Humans Suck! comic book mini-series issues 1 and 2

Oh My Goth! Graphic Novel

Oh My Goth! Graphic Novel Version 2.0

The Girls of Goth pinup book

Deady, The Malevolent Teddy Graphic Novel
(Sirius Entertainment)

Chi-Chian The Roleplaying Game
(Aetherco/Dreamcatcher)

Discography:

The Devil's Bris

Almost Human

Banned on Vulcan

Boo Hoo

Then and Again

(Projekt Records)

To Our Readers

Weiser Books, an imprint of Red Wheel/Weiser, publishes books across the entire spectrum of occult and esoteric subjects. Our mission is to publish quality books that will make a difference in people's lives without advocating any one particular path or field of study. We value the integrity, originality, and depth of knowledge of our authors.

Our readers are our most important resource, and we appreciate your input, suggestions, and ideas about what you would like to see published. Please feel free to contact us, to request our latest book catalog, or to be added to our mailing list.

Red Wheel/Weiser, LLC
P.O. Box 612
York Beach, ME 03910-0612
www.redwheelweiser.com